Maritime Alderney

Victor Coysh

A Guernsey Press Publication

List of Illustrations

P.S. *Queen of the Isles*	6
Model of S.S. *Courier*	8
Trinity House ship *Patricia*	11
S.S. *Staffa*	12
Loss of H.M.S. *Victory*	22
Loss of *Petite Raymond*	27
Loss of *Leros*	28
Loss of *Rhenania*	29
H.M.S. *Anson*	33
H.M.S. *Alderney*	34
Casquets lighthouse	36
Alderney lighthouse	39

(The cover illustration is of the wreck of the *Liverpool*, from a painting by Charles Jacques, reproduced by kind permission of the Guernsey Post Office Board, who also permitted the use of the drawing of *H.M.S. Alderney*, by A. D. Theobald).

© Victor Coysh 1991

All rights reserved. No part of this publication may be reproduced, stored in a retrieval system, or transmitted, in any form or by any means, electronic, mechanical, photocopying, recording or otherwise, without the prior permission of Victor Coysh

First published 1991

Made and printed in Great Britain by
The Guernsey Press Co. Ltd, Guernsey, Channel Islands.

ISBN 0 902550 43 8

Contents

Introduction	4
Prehistoric Craft	4
Medieval Ships	5
Victorian Shipping	7
The Couriers	8
Other Steamers	10
Trinity House Ships	11
Ships of the Occupation	13
Post-war Vessels	14
Trading and other Craft	15
Life-boats	17
Wrecks	18
The Navy at Braye	32
Yachting	34
Lighthouses	36
Ship Index	40

Introduction

TODAY, most people bound to and from Alderney travel by aircraft and, as a result, the island is linked with the United Kingdom, Guernsey, Jersey and France as it never was before. At the same time, nearly all its commodities must travel by sea, since the aeroplanes in service cannot carry coal, oil, cement, vehicles and other heavy cargo, all of which have to be imported by ship.

This book attempts to tell of vessels, large and small, which have served Alderney over the past centuries. The island's maritime history is as long as it is colourful, so medieval sailing ships, privateers' and smugglers' craft, cutters, paddle steamers, warships — these and many more receive attention by the author.

The shores of Alderney are both attractive and deadly and their 'wreck record' is high. Sometimes, when the island has been shrouded in fog, ships have lost their bearings in poor visibility, or have ventured too near, with the result that fierce currents have swept them onto reefs, to their doom. Wrecks have been especially numerous off Burhou, Braye, Mannez and Longis. Some have been refloated, but most ended their days on the Alderney coast.

In preparing this book, I have been helped by David Couling's *'Wrecked in the Channel Islands'*, by Louisa Lane Clarke's *Alderney Guide* and I have consulted my own little works, *Afoot in Alderney* and *Channel Islets*. The 'Guernsey Evening Press & Star' has also been of assistance, as well as my friend, Brian Bonnard, of Alderney.

Prehistoric Craft

IN the opinion of Dr John Renouf, expressed in his book, *The First Farmers of the Channel Islands,* Alderney became an island in about 7000 BC. Hitherto it had been part of the Continental mainland, like its fellows. It was also his view that at approximately the same period people first came to Alderney. They arrived, he believed, in skin-covered boats from the Cotentin Peninsula, and their objective was the cultivation of the soil. Some authorities believe that the relatively large number of prehistoric graves in the Islands suggested their original sanctity — *Isles of the Blest* — and hold that the folk so entombed were notables from the Continent, rather than local worthies. If this be so, obviously boats must have been used to carry the remains across the Race.

Little is known of the period between the New Stone Age and the possible establishment of a Roman Station at Longis, Alderney's original port. Archaeologist David Johnston, in his work, *The Channel*

Islands, an Archaeological Guide, believes there was a harbour there in Roman times, which was used "at least until the late Middle Ages". The remains of a stone jetty survive to this day on the western side of Longis Bay. Other historians share this view, although the story that the port was abandoned because of a sandstorm at some unspecified period is disbelieved. It is far more likely that Longis Bay and Harbour gradually silted up, commerce between that port and Normandy faded, and Braye became the Island's port from 1736 onwards.

Medieval Ships

IN the so-called Dark Ages, knowledge of Alderney's history is meagre, and still less is known of the ships that called here. Clearly, fishing craft used Longis and other relatively safe harbours from time immemorial, but regular services between the Island and France, England and the other Channel Islands came much later. In *A People of the Sea* (edited by A. G. Jamieson), there is mention of John Le Bere, master of the *George* of Alderney in 1471. At this time there was considerable trading between the Islands and Poole.

Smugglers used the Island extensively and their boats must have been familiar sights to Alderney folk, many of whom were closely involved in the "Free Trade" which, in the Islands, was not illegal. The era of privateering brought further wealth to Alderney, and some of the ships so engaged were locally owned.

One, the *Resolution,* brought its owners John and Henry Le Mesurier, £134,589 in prize moneys, and this, in the 18th Century, was a fortune. It was thanks to privateering that the old jetty at Braye was built in 1736.

Another, the Cutter *Hope,* was given a warrant by the Governor, Peter Le Mesurier, in 1793 to 'cruize round the said Island' and act as a 'Spy Cutter to watch the Motions of the Enemy', the owner, Mr John Samford, to be paid £60 per month for the hire of his vessel and crew.

John Jacob, in his *"Annals" of the Bailiwick of Guernsey* (published in 1830), travelled from Guernsey to Alderney by fishing boat, suggesting that, when he was writing the book, there was no regular communication between the islands. Yet, in J. T. Cochrane's *Guide to Guernsey* published in 1826, the cutters *Frederick* (Simon) and *Experiment* (Le Cocq) operated this service. The *Experiment* was still sailing in 1848, according to Louisa Lane Clarke's *Guide to Guernsey,* although by then a steamer service had been introduced as well.

MARITIME ALDERNEY

Queen of the Isles at St. Peter Port.

Victorian Shipping

IN 1847 work began on the building of the great breakwater at Braye, and there was need of a vessel to bring materials from Guernsey to Alderney. Jackson and Bean, the contractors, employed the paddle steamer *Princess Royal*, and she ran between the islands until 1853, when she was sold for £1,200. The iron-built *Queen of the Isles* succeeded her, and she operated the service until 1872, carrying passengers as well as cargo. These passengers were Alderney's first visitors, coming primarily to view the building work at Braye and the coastal forts also under construction.

The vessel's tonnage was 81, and she could carry 370 passengers (with berths for 25). The fares were 3s. 6d. and 2s. 6d., i.e. First and Second Class. The vessel's figurehead was that of Queen Victoria, and the ship was commanded by Capt. Scott, whose wife kept Scott's Hotel in Braye Road, for many years. Her husband commanded his paddle steamer when Queen Victoria visited Alderney in 1854 in the Royal Yacht *Victoria and Albert* (I). A fine painting by Paul Naftel shows the assembly of ships at Braye. It now hangs in the Queen's collection, but a modern print, and a contemporary engraving from one of Naftel's sketches for the original, are on display in the Alderney Society Museum.

Queen Victoria returned in 1857 aboard the second yacht of the same name. She saw the numerous defences, whose guns, ammunition and supplies formed part of the cargoes of War Department vessels from England.

Although the *Queen of the Isles* was disposed of in 1872, Scott and others believed there was the need for such a ship on the inter-island run, and they purchased the 100-ton *Princess*. However she was sold in 1875, also for £1,200, and for a while passengers and mail were carried to and from Guernsey by sailing cutter, as was the case before steamers were employed.

The *Couriers*

THE Alderney firm of Barbenson & Company resolved to improve matters by re-introducing a steamship service. Its principals, Judge Nicholas Barbenson, Capt. W. Whales and Messrs Blatchford, Cutler and Willis approached the Southampton shipbuilders Day & Summers, and ordered the construction of what was to become the screw steamer *Courier*.

She arrived at Braye for the first time in April 1876. Of 136 tons, this handsome, yacht-like little ship had a slim buff funnel and two masts on which sail was sometimes set. As well as carrying cargo she had attractive passenger accommodation, with "closet conveniences" for ladies and gentlemen. Her speed was 10 knots, powerful enough to tackle the Swinge, and, when Cherbourg bound, the Race.

After a few years her owners felt that, good though she was, something bigger was needed, so in 1883, a new *Courier* arrived in Alderney waters. Curiously enough both shared the same name without the addition of I or II and, as each resembled the other at a distance, confusion reigned at times, since the two steamers remained in service together for some years.

The "Big" *Courier*, as people called her, was of 151 tons, and certainly she was superior to the other ship. She was bigger, faster, had better accommodation for passengers, and so excellent a sea-

Model of Courier *in Alderney Society's Museum.*

boat was she, that she sailed in island waters for a great many years, often under appalling conditions. She also ran excursions to the other islands, as well as regularly calling at Cherbourg. On two occasions she was wrecked; once off Jethou, and more serious, when she sank off Sark. The "Little" *Courier* was sold in 1913, and her big sister was, for a while, the only vessel owned by what became known as The Alderney Steam Packet Company.

Often she assisted vessels in distress, especially in the days when Alderney lacked a lifeboat. In 1905 she struck the eastern pierhead of the New Harbour where she often coaled. She was beached at Braye, temporarily repaired, and then proceeded to Guernsey for further attention. While the *Courier* was out of action, the motor vessel *Lita* often replaced her. This craft ran the Casquets Lighthouse relief for a long period. During World War I the ship was painted grey, and once sighted a U-boat four or five miles off the Garden Rocks. There were times when the Guernsey-based French sea-planes escorted the little vessel between St Peter Port and Braye. Early in World War II the *Courier* was still operating, but the shadow of the German Occupation soon intervened. In June 1940 she left Braye with cattle for Guernsey, and later left again with passengers and pigs, and that was the last Alderney saw of her for five years.

During the war she was on Naval service, and in July 1947 was lying at Weymouth, for sale. Sark Projects Ltd purchased her for the Sark and Alderney service, and after an overhaul she passed down the Swinge, bound for Guernsey. She was a different *Courier* in appearance and some of her good looks had gone. She mounted topmasts, her funnel was white with a black top, and she had a new wheelhouse. The Royal Mail ornamental scrolls and bow decorations were no more, and she carried new boats.

Soon she was back on the Alderney service, but not for long. She was old and expensive to operate and her accommodation was not up to modern standards. All too soon she was withdrawn, and proceeded to Weymouth in the autumn of 1947 where she was once more offered for sale. Ultimately, this valiant ship was broken up in Holland in 1950.

A steamer rather resembling her was the *Serk* (originally the *Alert*), which sometimes replaced the *Courier* when she was under survey or repair. The *Serk* was built in 1885 and was based in Guernsey. One day, bound for Alderney, she spent many hours at anchor off the Garden Rocks in thick fog. On another occasion she was steaming up the Race towards Cherbourg with a deck load of hay, when she almost capsized in the rough sea, but ended her journey safely.

Other Steamers

ALDERNEY sometimes saw the s.s. *Fawn* built in 1897 and normally running between Guernsey and France. In 1923 she was replaced by the *New Fawn,* bigger but less attractive-looking, which figured in the evacuation of Alderney in 1940 when she took horses and cattle to Guernsey before steaming to England, having coaled at Braye first. She was the last Guernsey vessel to leave before the Occupation, and was later converted to a motor vessel.

In 1920, the Alderney Steam Packet Company bought the old paddle steamer *Helper,* primarily for the Guernsey–Sark service, but occasionally used on the Alderney run. She was broken up in 1926, and was replaced by the *Riduna* (ex HMS *Argus*). She resembled a steam-yacht with her clipper bow, buff funnel, and white hull, though later her colour scheme was changed. Her name was supposed to be that given to Alderney by the Romans, though most historians discredit this. Her stay in local waters was brief.

Although occasionally Alderney saw the former mail packet *Arpha,* she did not last long here. She ran excursions from Bournemouth to the Island in 1938 and 1939, and a year later her owners, Sark Motorships, disposed of her. She was the *Canterbury* originally, built in 1899 and with a tonnage of 561.

Another caller in the days prior to World War I, was the paddle steamer *Monarch,* a handsome vessel built in 1888 and owned by Cosens & Company, of Weymouth. She ran trips from Bournemouth to Alderney. The vessel was broken-up in 1950. There were times when Alderney's Garrison was changed, and often a railway mail steamer would bring troops to Braye, and take them away again in due course.

In the last century, if not earlier, a considerable number of cattle were exported to England, since farmers believed they would enrich the quality of thin milk, and because the gentry found them decorative. One of the ships employed in this industry was the former London & South-Western Railway's s.s. *Guernsey,* built in 1874 and with a tonnage of 280. Originally a passenger vessel, she was converted into a cargo boat. She was wrecked off Cap de la Hague in 1915.

Trinity House Ships

VESSELS of this Corporation have maintained lighthouses in the Guernsey Bailiwick for a great many years and they have been specially prominent in Alderney waters, periodically visiting the Casquets when maintenance or improvements were necessary. Of particular interest, as far as Alderney was concerned, was the presence of the *Vestal*, which took-off the Casquets keepers on June 21st, 1940, when it became obvious that the Germans were about to invade the Channel Islands, following their occupation of the nearby Cherbourg peninsula. The ship then called at Braye to collect the keepers of Mannez lighthouse and she arrived at dawn. As well as the lighthouse men the *Vestal* took aboard their families, three Trinity House pensioners and some civilians.

This episode is well told in Richard Woodman's *Keepers of the Sea*, he being a master of Trinity House vessels. The ship then proceeded to St Peter Port to embark Guernsey and Sark keepers and their families, and with 40 aboard she steamed to England. The *Vestal* was better remembered in the island when she was named *Patricia*, the handsome yacht used by the Elder Brethren of the Corporation on their annual inspection of the Guernsey Bailiwick lighthouses.

Trinity House yacht Patricia *in Alderney roadstead.*

She was more than a yacht, as were other ships so-named (including the earlier *Irene*), since they were used on maintenance duties when required. Other Trinity House vessels to visit Alderney include the *Alert, Beacon, Siren, Winston Churchill* and the *Stella*.

The mfv. *Burhou* was in the service of Trinity House and carried out the relief of keepers and conveyance of supplies for several years. Her skipper was Pilot Nick Allen, a well known Alderney character. Obviously heavy gear was taken to the lighthouse by Trinity House ships but, even then, the *Burhou* was used in conveying it from ship to rock. She began operating as soon as the lighthouse came under the control of Trinity House after the German Occupation and continued to do so until 1972 when helicopters replaced her. For several years her dinghy lay on the quayside of the New Harbour, long after Trinity House had disposed of the *Burhou*.

The steamer Staffa *at Braye in 1940.*

Ships of the Occupation

WHEN the bulk of the Island's population forsook Alderney on Sunday, June 23rd, 1940, they travelled to England aboard six ships which had arrived at Braye at the request of Judge F. G. French, the Civic Head of Alderney. On July 20th the m.v. *White Heather* conveyed a party of Guernseymen to clear up the disorder in Alderney following the hurried evacuation by the inhabitants, and to collect foodstuffs and other useful stores which had been abandoned. The vessel was a former Cornish fishing boat, more recently employed on service between Guernsey and Brecqhou. Later she ran between Guernsey and Alderney together with the *Staffa*.

The *Staffa* (90 tons) was acquired by J. B. Le Page of Guernsey in 1939 and was taken over by the Germans in 1940. They renamed her the *Xavier Dorsch*. In March 1943, she ran aground, having been blown off her moorings at Braye. She became a total loss, remaining on the rocks until 1951, when she was broken-up.

Several German-operated vessels were to be seen at Braye between 1940 and 1945, particularly during the period when the island was being fortified. Vast quantities of building materials were imported from France, and the commercial quay had to be lengthened with an iron extension which became unsafe and was demolished sometime after the war. As well as guns, mines and ammunition, troops were also carried aboard these ships, which were chiefly of French or Dutch origin, and of no special interest in appearance. Few German warships used the harbour, although there were small guard vessels based there. They were former French fishing boats, according to T. X. H. Pantcheff's Book, *Alderney, Fortress Island*. They also conveyed men and supplies to the Casquets, the lighthouse of which was operated by naval personnel. In 1944 the vessels which took away prisoners and labourers were named *Derflinger*, *Franka*, *Gerfried*, *Holstein*, *Klaus Wilhelm*, *Lena* and *Spinel*.

Post-War Vessels

FOLLOWING the Liberation of the Islands in May 1945, Alderney was visited by British Forces on May 16th, when a party arrived from Guernsey by naval craft. In December of that year the first exiled islanders returned in the *Autocarrier*, a Southern Railway ship which sometimes ran between Southampton and Guernsey. Kevin Le Scelleur, in his book, *Channel Island Railway Steamers*, states that she was built in 1931 and had a gross tonnage of 985. She was scrapped in 1954. His book has a photograph of the ship arriving at Braye with returning islanders, bunting flying from her masts.

The *Autocarrier* was escorted by two naval launches and she returned with more evacuees early in 1946. In March of that year the Great Western Railway ran a weekly cargo service from Weymouth to the island, but the ship operating it, the *Roebuck*, could only carry twelve passengers. With the gradual withdrawal of the Liberating Forces from Alderney, the use of naval vessels for civilian purposes came to an end.

One of the first ships to operate on the Guernsey-Alderney service after the Navy had left, was the ss. *Radford*, of 477 tons and built in 1935. She started work in 1948, but the service was unprofitable and she was soon withdrawn. Of much greater interest was her successor, the *Island Commodore*, a former torpedo recovery vessel, built in 1942 and of 195 tons. In 1948 Commodore Cruises, (a firm operating the Sark–Guernsey service), chartered her from the Ministry of Transport and she traded between Guernsey, Alderney, Sark and Poole. Later the company bought her, and the Poole service was abandoned. This staunch little ship was bought by the Isle of Sark Shipping Company in 1970 and was renamed *Ile de Serk*. She was sold in 1984 and sailed across the Atlantic to her new owners. In September, 1989, she was blown ashore in Dominica and was abandoned.

In the late 1940s both the *St. Julien* and *St. Helier* (Weymouth mailboats) ran excursions to Alderney from the Dorset port, but the Southampton registered *Brittany* was far better known here, both before and after World War II. Owned by the Southern Railway, she was built in 1933 and her tonnage was 1,445. In summer she was used on excursions between the Islands, and this handsome vessel was very popular. She was sold in 1963.

Another "Commodore" vessel to visit Alderney in 1947 and 1948 was the *Sark Coast*, a former landing craft, and used chiefly on the Guernsey–Sark service. Small coasters berthing at Braye in the 1950s included the *St. Ernest, Arrowhead, Herm Coast* and *Ridunian*. More recent were the *Alderney Courier* seen at Braye in the 1970s, *Alderney Trader* (1969-73), *Ord* (1975-1983), *Bandick* (built in 1961), *La Pia* (1979-1987), the *Carrigrennan* (1986-1989), and at intervals the *Mary Coast* (1987-1990). The port was sometimes visited by the *Sea Trent* (1974), and the coaster *Courier* in the 1980s. All these carried cargo only and had no passenger accommodation.

In 1988 the mv.*Seafox* began operating a service between Guernsey, Alderney and the Normandy ports of Goury and Dielette.

In 1981 Torbay Seaways started a service from Torquay to Guernsey, via Alderney. Their first ship the *Devoniun* (formerly the Scilly Isles' packet *Scillonian II*) arrived at Braye amidst a certain amount of rejoicing, since passenger ships were rarely seen there. She was withdrawn in 1984 and her successor was given the same name. Formerly she was the Scottish mailboat *Clansman,* and has a hydraulic lift allowing her to carry vehicles on a roll-on, roll-off basis.

Unhappily, Alderney is no longer served by hydrofoil. In 1987 a service was started from Torquay, but proved to be unacceptable in rough weather and was soon abandoned. Later, hydrofoils called at Alderney to and from Guernsey and Weymouth, but they no longer do so.

Great excitement was caused on the 22nd September, 1987 when the 8,000-ton Smyril Line cruise ship *Norona* put into Braye Bay for two days with a party of German tourists. She was the largest passenger ship ever to use Braye Harbour, and almost the entire population went down to Braye to see her. She is normally employed on Mediterranean and Atlantic cruises.

Trading and other craft

STONE was exported from the island on a relatively big scale from 1840-1940. Quarrying was an important industry, which really began when prodigious quantities of stone were needed for the construction of the Breakwater and Forts. Sailing craft loaded it from the old pier and from the breakwater, and later from the Cachalière pier on the south side of the island (built specially for this trade. It is now derelict). These vessels included Thames barges. One of the craft so engaged was the brig *Edissa,* owned by Nicholas Barbenson (a prominent islander), who also was the owner of the schooner-yacht *Ellen.*

Among the vessels formerly seen at Braye were the so-called "dynamite boats". Explosives needed for quarry blasting were brought to the island in relatively large steamers, and for safety's sake, they were transferred to smaller craft in the roadstead. An early edition of *The Channel Pilot* stated that whilst this operation was in progress, "very frequently a steamer lies in the roadstead at night with a red light on her foremast head." The mariner was cautioned not to mistake this for one of Braye's red leading lights. Other callers included War Department vessels bringing military requirements, and sometimes they were engaged in towing targets for the benefit of gunners manning the forts. The ships taking away stone often brought coal to the island, and this was normally discharged at the Douglas Quay and, later, at the commercial wharf built at the turn of the century.

In more recent times oil, rather than coal, has been of prime importance, and tankers are frequent callers, discharging their cargo through a fixed pipeline to the tanks behind the generating station in York Hill Quarry.

In summer especially, sail training vessels now grace the port, and to observe the brig *Royalist,* and the tops'l schooners *Sir Winston Churchill, Malcolm Miller* and *Lord Nelson* (barque) approaching Braye with all sail set is a memorable sight. They, and the training ships of the Island Training Association in some measure recapture the days when wind-driven craft were a common sight.

Another bygone delight was to stand on the Butes, or Platte Saline and watch great liners steam by, bound to and from Cherbourg. The most notable were the Cunarders *Queen Mary* and *Queen Elizabeth.* Some Alderney pubs exhibited timetables of when these vessels were due to pass by, for the benefit of observers. The Butes was also the place to see a host of other ships, sailing or steaming, up or down the Channel. In the 1970s because of the volume of traffic in the Channel, for safety reasons, fixed shipping lanes were instituted which had the effect of taking the vessels much further out, they can now only be seen nearer the horizon on their eastward journeys, and the traffic largely consists of the Ro-Ro Ferries to Guernsey and Jersey (still referred to locally as 'the mailboats'), large and small container ships and tankers, and the occasional oil-rig and warships.

A sight now very seldom enjoyed is that of a large craft using the Swinge, a feat performed by railway steamers occasionally, as they sometimes used the Ortac passage, but a regular sight nowadays is the huge black and white French tug *Etoile de Languedoc* which is employed in policing and protecting the "lanes" between the Casquets and the Channel Light Vessel, and which frequently comes close in shore for protection in severe weather, sometimes passing through the Swinge.

Lifeboats

THE seas around Alderney are perilous indeed, and it is not surprising to learn that as long ago as 1869 a lifeboat was based on Braye. She was the *Mary and Victoria* (according to Guy Blampied's book, *Mayday, Mayday*), a ten-oared pulling and sailing boat. However she was very seldom used and the station was abandoned. This is not to say that there was no need for rescue craft here, but the type of boat employed was unsuitable for the troubled waters awaiting her. Ships in distress were often dealt with by Alderney fishing boats, and what valuable service they gave freely and with great courage! After motor lifeboats became based on Guernsey they usually went to vessels in trouble off Alderney, as did French rescue craft.

By the 1980s the number of yachts using the English Channel was very high, and they included scores of pleasure craft owned by Channel Islanders. Some of their skippers took unnecessary risks, either through bravado or ignorance, and the time came when the Royal National Lifeboat Institution in response to the appeals of the islanders led by Dr J. Ayoub, resolved to base a boat on Alderney again, on an experimental basis. She was the Brede class, *Forester's Future* which took up moorings at Braye in the spring of 1984. Almost at once her presence was justified and she was in practically constant demand. Ultimately the R.N.L.I. decided to make the base permanent and, in the autumn of 1986, the boat was replaced by the bigger Waveney class, *Louis Marchesi of Round Table*, whose record to date is truly excellent. There are now handsome new R.N.L.I. headquarters on Braye quayside. There are times when the lifeboats of Alderney operate jointly, in co-operation with aircraft from R.N.A.S. Culdross, but usually the local craft is quite capable of coping with "those in peril on the sea".

An impressive list of rescues has been built up since the re-establishment of the station in 1984.

The Wrecks

Numbers after ship's names refer to their approximate wreck positions on map.

LYING just off the main stream of traffic in the English Channel, beset by savage tides and formidable rocks, it is small wonder that Alderney's coast and its outliers have been the scene of countless shipwrecks. Added to these natural hazards, the absence of radio, radar and, indeed, warning lights — until relatively recently — made the island a place to be shunned unless, of course, a vessel were bound there. Even today, with so many aids to navigation available, the mariner should treat Alderney with respect and approach its shores with caution. Within the scope of this book one can but mention a handful of wrecks and the most spectacular of these have been selected. In a wreck list compiled by Eric Sharp about 30 years ago, nearly 200 were recorded off Alderney and, he stated, 'they represent but a fraction of the whole'.

Pioneer

A little vessel which played a not unimportant role in Alderney's maritime history was the ss. *Pioneer*, of 47 tons. Her owner was a Guernseyman named Martel, who specialised in wreck salvage in the early years of the present century. Illustrations of the ship are scarce, but she is partly visible in a photograph of the ss. *Rhenania*, wrecked off Burhou in 1912. The *Pioneer* is to be seen alongside the stricken vessel, looking small by comparison and with her single mast and tall funnel in view.

The *Pioneer* figured in the salvage of the cargo of the full-rigged ship *Liverpool*, lost off Alderney in 1902. Relics of the wreck, taken to Guernsey by the little steamer, were to be seen until recently at Martel's home, Les Pelleys, Castel and they included a windlass and the ship's name-plates. The *Pioneer* also assisted in the building of Guernsey's Platte Fougère lighthouse in 1909.

Perhaps her most interesting commission occurred in 1911, when George Sharp made an important decision in his life-style. He was one of the first to board the *Liverpool*, having lived near the scene of her stranding. He worked at Mannez quarry and his home almost adjoined it.

Tiring of working as a quarryman, George Sharp paid a visit to Sark in September, 1911, where he obtained permission from the Seigneur to rent the adjoining island of Brecqhou. Two months later he moved from Alderney aboard the chartered *Pioneer*, whose skipper's name was O'Connor. The ship carried all that George possessed, including cattle, pigs, a horse, a dog, fowls and, of course, dairy and farming implements and furniture! Also aboard was food for his household and livestock. The human element aboard comprised George, his brother, a carpenter and two nephews.

Happily, Sharp wrote a booklet about Brecqhou, which he sold to those who visited it and his description included this account of his voyage from one island to another. It is quite likely that, having been employed by the Admiralty at Mannez quarry, he obtained permission to move all his possessions by rail to Braye harbour, although he does not mention this in his brochure. He wrote of the good send-off he received at the harbour and of the fine weather encountered en voyage. Fog prevented the ship from reaching Brecqhou that day and she anchored off Sark until the next morning, when she anchored in Le Port and her human beings, animals and goods and chattels were unloaded. Sharp lived there for several years before taking up residence in Sark, where he died at a ripe old age.

Michael[2]

It was in 1701 that what may well be the first wreck to be recorded in Alderney waters occurred. It was that of the sailing vessel *Michael*, which struck the Casquets in the days before a lighthouse stood there. There were, however, two wooden huts on the rocks — perhaps a refuge for shipwrecked mariners — and some of the crew managed to take shelter there. Here they remained for many days, gradually starving to death. How they were saved smacks of the miraculous.

A lad aboard a Lymington ship had a dream and in it he saved a party of men on the Casquets. He told his father about it, but of course it was deemed but an idle dream. Yet as the ship neared the rocks, sailing from Guernsey, the crew observed the survivors and they were taken off, despite a rough sea, but only in the nick of time.

HMS Victory[1]

It was in October, 1744, that Admiral Balchen's flagship, *Victory*, was in Alderney waters with a fleet of 23 sail. A severe gale smote the vessels and *Victory* was ripped apart when she struck the Black Rock, part of the Casquets group. At the time no light shone there and on that night of storm the great ship was lost with all hands. Over 1,000 perished.

Several days elapsed before the Admiralty became aware of the disaster. Then came news that alarm guns had been heard firing

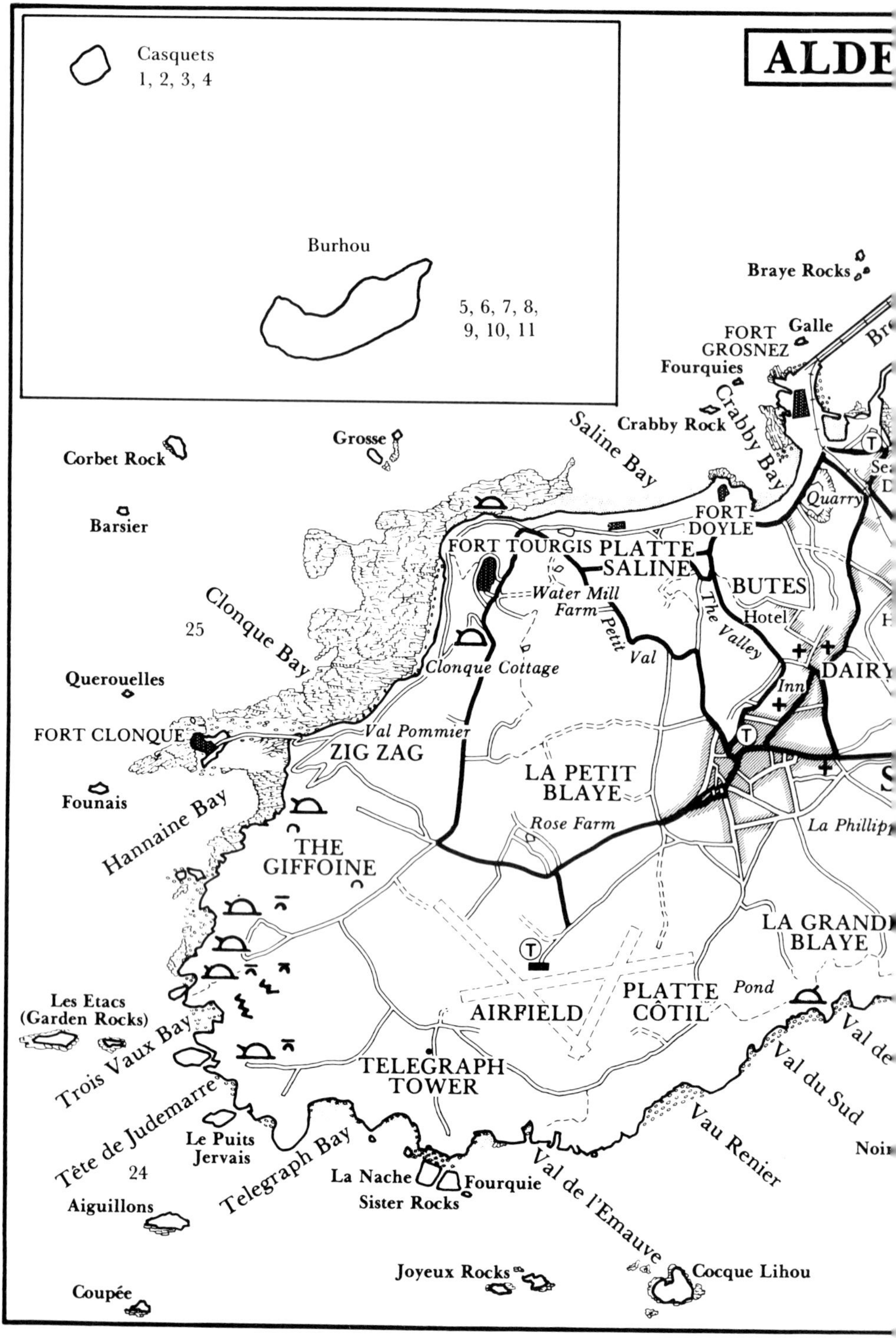

ALDE
Casquets
1, 2, 3, 4
Burhou
5, 6, 7, 8,
9, 10, 11
Braye Rocks
FORT GROSNEZ
Galle
Fourquies
Crabby Rock
Crabby Bay
Saline Bay
Corbet Rock
Grosse
Barsier
Quarry
FORT DOYLE
FORT TOURGIS
PLATTE SALINE
BUTES
Water Mill Farm
Petit Val
The Valley
Hotel
DAIRY
Inn
Clonque Bay
25
Clonque Cottage
Querouelles
FORT CLONQUE
Val Pommier
ZIG ZAG
LA PETIT BLAYE
Rose Farm
La Phillip
Founais
Hannaine Bay
THE GIFFOINE
LA GRAND BLAYE
Pond
PLATTE CÔTIL
AIRFIELD
Les Etacs (Garden Rocks)
Trois Vaux Bay
TELEGRAPH TOWER
Val de
Val du Sud
Vau Renier
Tête de Judemarre
Le Puits Jervais
24
Telegraph Bay
La Nache
Fourquie
Sister Rocks
Val de l'Emauve
Aiguillons
Joyeux Rocks
Cocque Lihou
Coupée
Noir

Map of Alderney

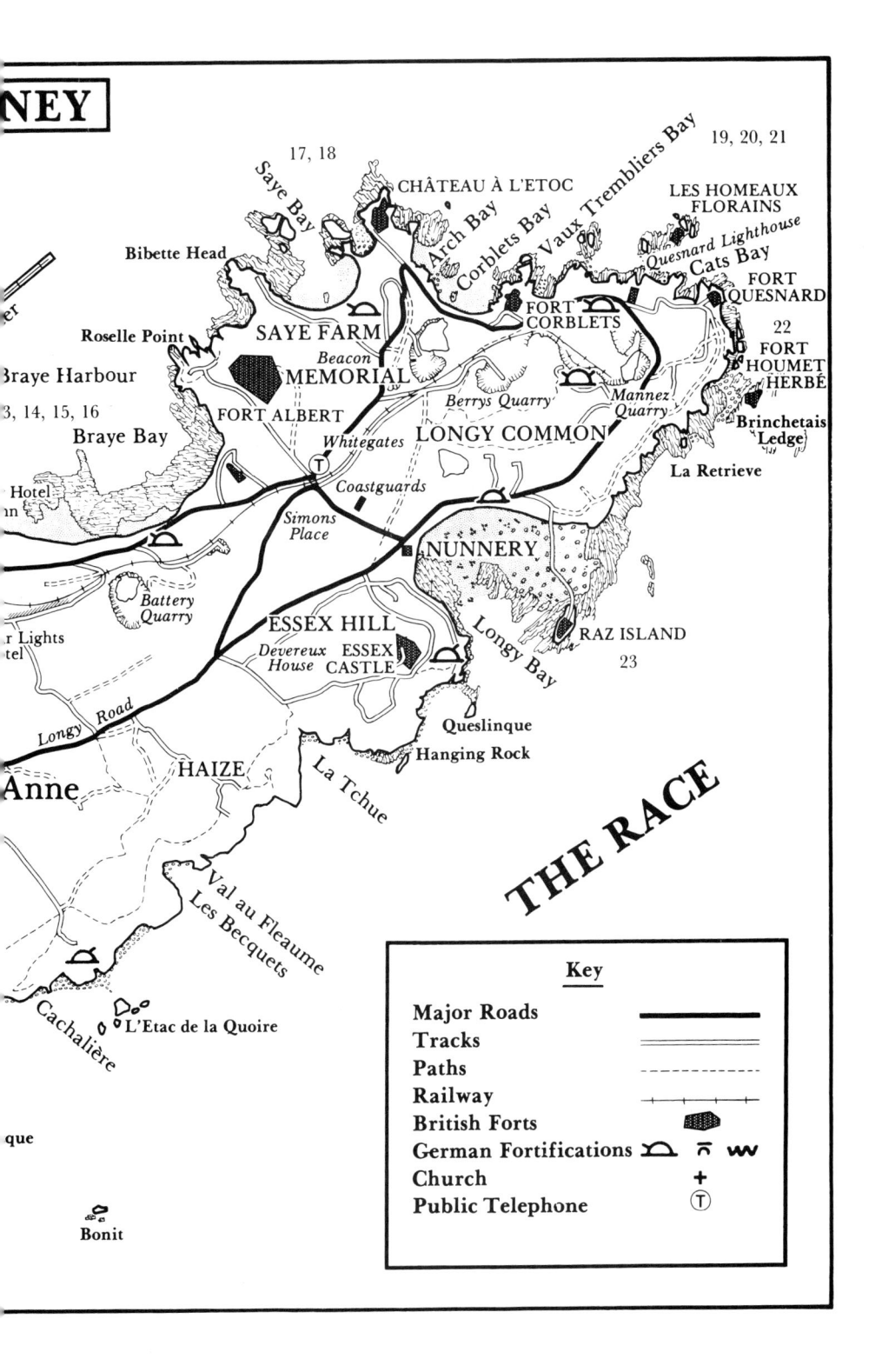

NEY

17, 18
19, 20, 21

Saye Bay
CHÂTEAU À L'ETOC
Arch Bay
Corblets Bay
Vaux Trembliers Bay
LES HOMEAUX FLORAINS
Bibette Head
Quesnard Lighthouse
Cats Bay
FORT CORBLETS
FORT QUESNARD
Roselle Point
SAYE FARM
22
Beacon
FORT HOUMET HERBÉ
Braye Harbour
MEMORIAL
Berrys Quarry
Mannez Quarry
3, 14, 15, 16
FORT ALBERT
LONGY COMMON
Brinchetais Ledge
Braye Bay
Whitegates
La Retrieve
Hotel
Coastguards
Simons Place
NUNNERY
Battery Quarry
Lights
ESSEX HILL
RAZ ISLAND
tel
Devereux House
ESSEX CASTLE
Longy Bay
23
Longy Road
Queslinque
Anne
HAIZE
Hanging Rock
La Tchue

THE RACE

Val au Fleaume
Les Becquets

Cachalière
L'Etac de la Quoire

que

Bonit

Key

Major Roads	━━━
Tracks	═══
Paths	- - -
Railway	┼┼┼
British Forts	▰
German Fortifications	⌒ ┬ w
Church	+
Public Telephone	Ⓣ

An imaginary picture by Peter Monamy of the wreck of H.M.S. Victory *off Les Casquets in 1744.*

in the vicinity of the Casquets and warships were despatched to investigate. They found wreckage from the flagship and this confirmed her loss.

HMS Amethyst[13]
From *The Edinburgh Evening Courant* of Jan. 7, 1796.

We are sorry to confirm the loss of the *Amethyst* frigate. She sailed from Torbay on Monday afternoon last, in company with the *Trusty*, on a cruize in the Channel. Early in the night she missed the Commodore's lights and by the severe gale of wind which then raged, she was driven on the Hannouaux (Hanois) rocks, near Guernsey, where she struck on Tuesday morning at four o'clock, and having got off from thence, was driven upon the island of Alderney and at half past nine ran on shore in the bay of Braye in that island.

It was luckily near high water and by waiting till the water was low, the crew were safely landed without losing a man. The three masts and bowsprit are gone, but if the weather proves moderate the stores will probably be saved. The people of Alderney were extremely earnest in carrying warps and messengers to the ship, but the sea ran so very high that they could not get near her, excepting one boat which got under her quarter and near enough to catch a rope, but was unfortunately overset and two of the men were drowned. The four others were saved by the great exertion of their friends on shore, who made a chain of persons, through a most tremendous surf, to rescue them. The sailors' clothes and bedding were all saved, and having their pockets full of money, very little regulation can take place among them so long as it lasts...

(N.B. Some bollards at Braye and Little Crabby harbour are said to have been cannon from the frigate).

Cimoni[14]

The looting of wrecks was all too popular among Alderney folk (and it was equally so elsewhere) and it was especially evident when, in a November gale in 1825, a Greek warship came to grief. She was the brig *Cimoni* and while the crew of forty came ashore safely, their reception was anything but cordial. A crowd of men, women and children had gathered on the beach and the valuables which were washed ashore were seized with such savagery that the captain declared that 'had I been cast ashore among Turks I should have expected death and met it; among Christians, from them I expected pity and protection. I have met with robbery instead.'

The Lieutenant-Governor, Sir John Colborne, hearing of this behaviour, went to Alderney, accompanied by Elisha Tupper, who spoke Greek. The captain, meeting the Guernsey party, said they behaved like angels rather than men! The crew were provided with food and clothing and each was presented with £5. The British Government also helped by sending HMS *Aurora* to take the shipwrecked men to Portsmouth, after they had spent Christmas in Guernsey. As for the valuables washed ashore, some were buried on the beach and some found their way to St Anne's.

Jupiter[17]

Helping oneself to a wreck's cargo often occurred in the past and it was especially evident when the Danish brig *Jupiter* came to grief here in 1833. She was bound from Hamburg to Valparaiso and went ashore on the north-east coast, a favourite site for wrecks. Although troops were sent to protect her valuable cargo, they were unequal to the task, since a great number of islanders swarmed to the scene and many came ashore from the ship with much loot. The soldiers resisted sampling the liquor aboard, unlike the civilians, several of whom were apprehended and jailed.

Carioca[18]

A dramatic event took place on an October night in 1865 off Chateau à l'Etoc, when this French barque was wrecked in a near hurricane. While in the Race she was blown on a lee shore after an abrupt change of wind, and she was dismasted. As she neared the rocks three men scrambled ashore and aroused the fort's guard. More help was forthcoming from troops at Fort Corblets and, in darkness, rain and wind, they set about rescuing the crew. Twenty-one were saved and the soldiers' gallantry was appropriately recognised. The storm raged for several days and two other French vessels were also lost off Alderney as a result, and with no survivors.

Behira[20]

Near Mannez lighthouse is the ruined fort of Les Homeaux Florains, standing on an islet and the scene of a wreck in March, 1895. It was that of the Glasgow steamer *Behira*, laden with coal, which struck the rocks in adverse weather. She sailed the seas no more.

Marie Fanny[5]

On a stormy night in December, 1896, two men were on Burhou, where they had been shooting. The weather prevented them from leaving and they went to sleep in the cottage there. In the early hours they heard a knock at the door and they were terrified. Burhou can be an eerie place at night and perhaps they believed a ghost was waiting outside. However, the knocking persisted and, on opening the door, they found a man on hands and knees, with a dog beside him. He said he was the master of the French steamer *Marie Fanny* and believed he was the sole survivor. All hands had been swept overboard as they attempted to launch the ship's boats. Happily the captain was wrong and some of the crew were saved, but 14 died and the bodies of nine of them were found at daybreak.

Stella[3]

Perhaps the most tragic wreck to have occurred in the Channel Islands happened on Good Friday, 1899, when the London & South-Western Railway Company's mail steamer *Stella* struck the Casquets and foundered, with great loss of life. Only nine years old, the ship was of 1,059 tons gross. She sailed from Southampton with 174 passengers and a crew of 43. As she approached the Casquets she ran into thick fog, but the captain did not reduce speed and she struck the Black Rock with considerable force. In those days there was intense rivalry between the masters of the Southampton and Weymouth packets. To them speed was of the essence and it was only after the *Stella* calamity that common sense prevailed and caution was observed in adverse weather conditions.

The vessel sank in eight minutes, allowing time for only four of her boats to be launched. There were 112 survivors, excluding the captain and a stewardess, Mrs Mary Rogers, who gave her life jacket to a passenger and refused to take her place in an already crowded boat. Some survivors were picked up by the ss. *Honfleur* and the Weymouth mail boat *Lynx*, but this was not until several hours after the ship foundered. It is curious that nobody aboard heard the Casquets foghorn (which had been blowing), neither did the keepers observe the ship's plight.

HMS *Viper*[6]

One of the most famous of Alderney's wrecks was that of this destroyer, brand new and one of the many warships engaged in the 1901 manoeuvres of the Channel Fleet. She was the first turbine-driven destroyer to be built for the Navy and her speed was 37 knots, making her the fastest vessel in the Fleet. In August, 1901, *Viper* was among the warships exercising in the Casquets waters.

Thick fog made visibility almost nil, but the vessel was still travelling at 22 knots when she struck the Renonquet reef, a mass of rocks close to Burhou. The strong tide swept the destroyer bumping from rock to rock until she stopped, capsized and broke in two. There was no loss of life, but this vitally important unit of the Royal Navy was a complete "write-off" and such a secret was made of her engines that parts of them were destroyed as the wreck lay on the rocks. Much of her armament was removed and the remains were sold to a Southampton firm, but they still lie where the disaster occurred on this lone outlier of Burhou.

Liverpool[21]

Beyond doubt, this, to date, has been the most outstanding of Alderney wrecks, partly because of her cargo, which islanders saved from the hands of authority, and because of her size and majestic appearance. It was early on a November day, in 1902, that John Godfray, bound for work in Mannez quarry, observed something very strange in the foggy conditions prevailing. It was the sight of a great ship ghosting along close by, only to be lost in the mist almost at once.

The man continued on his way, but at midday he heard voices in the fog which seemed to be coming from the fort on Homeaux

Florains islet, nearby. He thereupon launched his boat and rowed towards the rocks and there he saw the *Liverpool*, stranded, but with all sail still set. At the time she was the largest four-masted full-rigged ship in the world. With a tonnage of 3,300 she was 333 feet long and her great masts and yards were painted white. Her hull was grey, with black and white topsides. The ship was bound from Antwerp to San Francisco with a large and valuable general cargo.

Her master, unaware of her plight, ordered soundings to be taken and after finding six feet of water in her holds he ordered the crew to the boats. He had supposed the ship was in the vicinity of the Casquets and was unaware of the fact that strong tides and almost nil visibility had lured the great vessel to her doom off Alderney's formidable coast.

Naturally, the news of the wreck spread rapidly and soon crowds began to gather. They did more than stand and stare: they boarded the *Liverpool* with a view, perhaps, of lightening her of her cargo and maybe ensuring that it did not fall into unwelcome hands. They found she carried all manner of foodstuffs, intoxicants, silks and, less interesting, marble, cement, coke and girders. Today access to Homeaux Florains is extremely difficult, but in 1902 a causeway led from the shore to the fort and this the 'visitors' used.

Not only Alderney folk came to look and take, for excursions were run from Guernsey by the *Courier* and *Alert*, while the salvage vessel *Pioneer* was also involved. Photographs were taken and many an island home had (and has) relics of that fantastic windfall. Gradually the ship began to break up and her remains were sold to a syndicate. What remained of her cargo was sold for about £10,000 and much of it was taken to Guernsey. Oddly enough, the graveyard of the *Liverpool* was also that of other vessels.

Among them was that of the *Behira*, lost there in 1895 and, ten years later, that of the ss. *Portsea*.

Petit Raymond[19]
It was in 1906 that the French schooner so-named grounded near Homeaux Florains and became a total loss. She came to grief in a September gale while on passage from St Brieuc to Southampton with a cargo of potatoes. All the crew, except the master, reached the shore safely, although he had to be forcibly removed from ship to lifeboat. Coastguards assisted in the rescue and, to avoid pilfering (doubtless with memories of the *Liverpool* in this respect), troops from the garrison mounted guard night and day. This seems rather odd, for who would bother about potatoes after the riches of the bigger ship had been sampled?

MARITIME ALDERNEY

Wreck of Petite Raymond, *1906.*

Wreck of Leros *in 1906.*

Leros[7]

The year 1906 saw another Alderney shipwreck, this time off Burhou. It occurred in May and this German steamer, of 7,500 tons, had numerous sewing machines in her cargo. As usual, many islanders 'assisted' in removing them and soon the Burhou shore was covered with them. It is said that an individual sold the machines for five shillings each, to the chagrin of the Singer Sewing Machine Company's representative, when he arrived on the scene.

The *Leros* became a total loss and was blown up where she had stranded. Her engines, however, were salvaged. It is said that her crew refused assistance when approached by a local fisherman, but when the Germans finally took to the boats they found the bungs had been removed. The boats began to sink, the crew cried for help and were glad to welcome the man whom they had earlier repulsed.

Lynn O'Dee[8]

Burhou was again the scene of a shipwreck when, in June, 1910, this steamer came to grief, becoming a total loss — a fate all too often experienced on the Alderney coast. A small vessel, she was bound for Guernsey in ballast when fog drove her ashore, after striking La Lague ledge. The crew took to the boats and landed in Corblets bay and later the ss. *Courier* conveyed them to Guernsey.

Felix de Absalo[23]

The year 1910 was something of a vintage one for wrecks. In June the steamer *Rap*[13] was lost after she had struck the Pierres du Butes, a reef near Burhou. She broke in two, but happily the crew, in their boats, were towed to safety by the pilot launch *Lita*. At about the same time the ss. *Terra* came to grief and, unhappily for the owners, both she and the *Rap* belonged to the same company.

The June of that year saw much fog and this was the cause of these two wrecks and led to yet another at the same period.

The *Felix de Absalo*, a Spanish steamer, stranded on the Boufresses reef, near Raz Island, after losing her bearings in the Race. High and dry, this 2,076-ton vessel broke her back and became a total loss. Troops from Fort Albert saved the crew and also the captain's wife, who had given birth only the day before. The ship made an impressive sight, high and dry on Longis beach, but all too soon she disappeared.

Burton[12]

During 1911 there were further Alderney wrecks and Braye beach presented the unusual picture of two vessels ashore within a few hundred yards of each other. One was the ss. *Burton*, which had left Braye in January, laden with stone. Soon afterwards she struck the Grois reef, damaging her hull. The *Courier* went to her assistance and towed her back to Braye, where she was beached. Soon afterwards she broke her back.

The other Braye wreck was that of the Thames barge *Charles Ellison*[16]. She, too, had loaded stone at Braye but later broke from her moorings and drifted onto rocks in the bay. The crew were saved, but not their ship.

Rhenania[9]

La Lague reef, near Burhou, was responsible for the end of this Dutch steamer of 1,600 tons and again fog was the culprit. The disaster happened in April, 1912, when the ship was bound for Spain with general cargo and cattle. Her master, crew and some of the animals landed on Burhou, where the cattle remained for three weeks. They were in the care of the mate, who lived in the cottage. Some cattle were drowned in the ship's hold, but her cargo was salvaged, thanks to the crew, who prevented looting. As was the

Rhenania *wrecked off Burhou in 1912, with* Pioneer *alongside.*

fate of so many other ships, the *Rhenania* never sailed the seas again. She attracted many spectators, some of whom travelled from Guernsey, where excursions were organised to view her plight. Some of her relics travelled to Guernsey, including her funnel, bell and an ornate mirror.

Emily Eveson[25]
Those who stroll along the road to Clonque at low tide may notice a ship's boiler at the northern end of the beach. It came from this smart little coaster of 630 tons, which was stranded in this bay in May, 1922, becoming, as usual, a total loss. The incident was rather dramatic, for at midnight the crew took to the boats and, before landing, they cried for help. This aroused a dog at Clonque Cottage, whose barking awakened the occupants. They guided the crew to safety, although at first they feared the men were intruders.

Later that morning the *Courier* was steaming down the Swinge when her master noticed the plight of the *Emily Eveson*. On arrival at Guernsey he reported the matter to the harbourmaster. Meanwhile, the crew were treated most hospitably by the Mignots, of Clonque Cottage, and by the people of St Anne's.

Empress[15]
One stormy day in February, 1923, this sailing barge was seeking shelter in Braye harbour when, on rounding the breakwater, she missed stays and could not come about. Her master anchored and discharged distress signals and to her rescue went pilot Vic Petit and his crew. He invited the men of the barge to abandon ship, but this they declined. The skipper wanted the Trinity House ship *Warden* (at Braye at the time) to tow the *Empress* clear of the roads, but the captain refused, because of the gale. The barge dragged her anchor and drifted near the rocks. Under truly dreadful conditions pilot Petit rescued the crew, but the operation took over four hours. For this he received the Lloyds Medal for saving life. The barge foundered soon after her crew had left her.

Edirne[10]
This vessel, of 3,653 tons, with a crew of 50, went aground on a reef near Burhou in fog early in 1950 and this relatively large number of people were rescued by the St Peter Port lifeboat *Queen Victoria*. They and their dog were taken off this badly damaged vessel, after the lifeboatmen had found 20 men in one of the ship's boats, the remainder having gone ashore. The *Queen Victoria* proceeded to Guernsey, towing three of the empty boats, but was obliged to abandon them because of worsening weather. Later,

an attempt was made to tow the *Edirne* off the reef, but although this was achieved she later foundered in deep water.

Constantia S[4]

This tanker, bound for Gibraltar with a cargo of fresh water, was lost on the Casquets on January 23, 1967. A vessel of 8,686 tons, was sighted by RMS *Sarnia* lying on the rocks with a heavy list and pounded by rough seas. The captain had clambered onto the rocks, while the crew took to the boats. The mail steamer and other vessels stood by and a RAF aircraft and a French helicopter were in attendance.

The *Sarnia* was brought as close to the rocks as possible while hot drinks and blankets were prepared for the crew. Rope ladders were lowered and despite the rolling of the ship in the rough sea the crew were saved. Also in attendance was the St Peter Port lifeboat *Euphrosyne Kendal* and her bow, at one stage of the operations, caught in the mail steamer's side. Happily, as the ship rose on a wave, the lifeboat was freed.

The tanker's boats were abandoned and the *Sarnia* steamed to Weymouth with ten rescued men aboard. The remainder of the crew, numbering 16, were picked up by the THV *Burhou*. The captain was taken off by French helicopter and taken to Guernsey. Ultimately, the ship broke in two and became a total loss.

Armas[11]

Of 2,545 tons, this Cypriot steamer struck rocks off Burhou on a November day in 1973. Two helicopters from HMS *Engadine* (which happened to be in the vicinity at the time) rescued the steamer's crew, although one man was drowned. The *Armas* remained high and dry for many months, but relentless seas gradually destroyed her and, ere long, she became yet another victim of the cruel coast of this island.

Point Law[24]

This coastal tanker of 1,500 tons had been a fairly regular visitor to the Channel Islands until she came to grief in dramatic circumstances on a July morning in 1975. She ran ashore near Le Puits Jervois, adjacent to Telegraph bay, and the wreck was easily viewed by many from the cliffs nearby. She was wedged firmly on the rocks, but her crew of twelve were rescued in an exciting and well-accomplished operation by the St Peter Port lifeboat *Sir William Arnold*, a French helicopter and the MFV *Christmas*. The Alderney fire brigade also assisted with the use of searchlights on the clifftop.

The rescue was a hazardous experience for all involved and the St Peter Port lifeboat men were decorated by the RNLI for their bravery. The tanker soon began to break up, thanks to heavy seas pounding her, and the wreck was subsequently sold for scrap. It is interesting to recall that the cover picture of the RNLI calendar for 1978 depicted, in colour, the tanker aground, the lifeboat and helicopter in action and the Garden Rocks in the background.

Corrina[22]

This motor coaster struck the rocks adjoining Fort Houmet Herbé early in 1985 and she remained in this position for several months, before being towed off. Many spectators viewed her at close quarters, for it was a simple matter to clamber over the beach to the fort, from whose ramparts the wreck was clearly visible. She had been a fairly frequent visitor to the Islands and, while the spectacle certainly interested many, it was, as well, a sad sight. No lives were lost and, for once, the stranded ship did not end her days on the Alderney coast.

In May, 1987, the Guernsey Post Office issued a very attractive series of stamps depicting some Alderney wrecks. The artist was Guernsey resident Charles Jaques. The ships selected were the *Liverpool* (11p), *Petit Raymond* (15p), *Maina* (29p), *Burton* (31p) and *Point Law* (34p). The *Maina* was a yacht which stranded on the breakwater rocks in 1910, but was refloated, having suffered no damage to her hull.

The Navy at Braye

ALDERNEY'S breakwater was intended to form part of a naval base, rather similar to Portland, with a large expanse of sheltered water in which a fleet could anchor. This did not come to pass, but Braye has been the venue of Royal Navy ships for a century or more, even if they do usually arrive singly, and their presence adds greatly to the port's appeal. To list them all would be impossible within the scope of this book, so only a few examples can be cited.

Certainly the most memorable occasion was in 1901, when scores of men-of-war belonging to the Channel Fleet cast anchor in the roadstead and beyond it. They were on a large scale exercise and Alderney hosted the smaller vessels, mainly torpedo craft. Similar manoeuvres took place in 1906, when 400 warships were engaged in the Channel and some of them used the roadstead. These were the only occasions when the breakwater justified its existence from a naval point of view.

Mention has been made of Royal yachts which visited Braye, and the custom continues in the reign of Queen Elizabeth II, whose *Britannia* brought Her Majesty and other members of the royal family to Alderney. She also came in 1949, as Princess Elizabeth, travelling in HMS *Anson*, a battleship, and the biggest warship ever seen off Braye.

During the middle of the 19th Century, the fishery protection gunboat *Dasher* frequently visited the island, sometimes with supplies for the garrison, and when engaged in surveying local waters. There is a Dasher Rock (submerged) between Burhou and the Casquets, and possibly it was charted aboard this vessel. Maybe she hit it!! *Dasher* was present on the two visits of Queen Victoria to Alderney.

In 1905 the Duke of Connaught arrived here aboard the cruiser HMS *Monmouth*. Royal Connaught Square commemorates the occasion. Another notable caller was the Admiralty yacht *Enchantress*. In recent years frigates have also been seen at Braye on many occasions. They include HMSs *Grenville, Wakeful* and *Venus*. Destroyers too, arrived on courtesy visits, or, like the frigates, when the Lieutenant-Governor paid the island a formal call. Among the minor warships to be seen here was the surveying vessel *Shackleton* in the 1950s.

It was in 1946 that the submarine HMS *Alderney* was completed, and not long afterwards she arrived at Braye, where a most cordial welcome awaited her. Her submerged displacement tonnage was 1,620, and she was armed with a 4" gun and ten torpedo tubes. Her last of several visits was in 1967. Soon afterwards she was scrapped. The submarine's bell, name plates, pennant and other relics are now on display in the Alderney Society's Museum.

In 1979 another HMS *Alderney* was built in Aberdeen, destined to be a fishery protection vessel like her sisters HMSs *Guernsey* and *Jersey*. In the same year, amid great rejoicing, she berthed at Braye,

H.M.S. Anson *off Alderney.*

H.M.S. *Alderney*

which she has continued to do from time to time, and especially during Alderney Week.

The first reference to a warship bearing the island's name was in 1729, but little is known of her. Another *Alderney* was built in 1734, a bomb-ketch mounting eight guns. In 1743 came another so-named, armed with 24 guns, to be followed by yet one more in 1756, with eight cannon aboard. For such a small island to have lent her name to six ships of the Royal Navy is, indeed, a signal honour.

Among merchant vessels bearing the name of Alderney was a steamship owned by the London & South-Western Railway, which was built in 1875. Her gross tonnage was 612, and she was a cargo vessel, ending her days in 1914. The *Isle of Alderney* (formerly the ss. *Devonia*) was built in 1906 and had a gross tonnage of 314. Carrying passengers and cargo, she was owned by the Anglo-French Steamship Company, of Guernsey. In 1936 the Guernsey Trading Company bought her and renamed her. She then traded between the Channel Islands and Poole until she was sold in 1946, and scrapped in 1952.

Yachting

PLEASURE craft are unlikely to have paid Alderney visits prior to the building of the breakwater, since before the 1840s Braye must have been a very exposed haven and Longis is no place for yachts. Indeed, the turmoil at Braye during the breakwater's construction would have deterred most yachtsmen, so it is likely that they only began coming to the island in any numbers from about 1870 onwards. Its situation is certainly convenient for those sailing south from such harbours as Southampton, Poole, Weymouth and Devon ports and many a yachtsman, bound for Guernsey or Jersey, has put into Braye as a welcome resting-place. The breakwater forms a stalwart shelter for craft anchored in the roadstead or moored closer in, and lordly steam yachts, splendid sailers and humbler craft have been welcome visitors for many years.

At the present time there are about 50 moorings for visitors, and when the wind blows strongly from the east or north-east yachts frequently anchor under the lee of Fort Albert. At Braye the yachtsman is well served. Here he may eat and drink most handsomely. Here too he may sleep in comfort, lay in stores, have a shower or do his laundry, take a stroll along the breakwater (on a placid day) or, stretching his legs a little more, make his way up to St Anne's. At the New Harbour (more properly known as Little Crabby Harbour), he will find a ship chandlery and facilities for fuelling and repairs.

That excellent maritime guide, *The Channel Pilot*, tends to alarm some yachtsmen with its references to strong tides, formidable rocks and other hazards off the Alderney coast, but, states the useful brochure, *Sailing to Alderney*, "If the unhandy vessels of the Victorian fleet could manage, so can an auxiliary yacht". It declares that while the island is a convenient 'stop-off' to and from France and the other Channel Islands, it is far more than that and the charms of Alderney are duly, and rightly extolled. This little book gives the yachtsman excellent counsel in respect of navigation, as does another pamphlet, *Alderney Sailing Directions.*

Local yachtsmen are well catered for by the Alderney Sailing Club whose comfortable headquarters stand beside the harbourmaster's office, on a rise between the Commercial Quay and the New Harbour. Close by is the R.N.L.I. crew station. The sailing club has over 600 members and visiting members of recognised yacht clubs are welcome to its hospitality.

From time to time Alderney ponders on the wisdom of creating a yacht marina at Braye, following the examples set by Guernsey and Jersey. At the time of writing, however, this development is no more than a pipe dream or, as some declare, a nightmare!

Lighthouses

The Casquets

THESE rocks, whereon the waves cascade (hence the name, some declare), must have been the bane of the Channel mariner since boats were invented. They stand on the fringe of this maritime highway and before a warning light shone from these Alderney outliers, countless craft must have come to grief there. They stand 90 feet above high water, right in the path of vessels bound to and from the Channel Islands and it was not until 1723 that some rudimentary steps were taken towards establishing a light on one of them.

In that year Thomas Le Cocq, of Alderney, received a licence to set up three coal fires within glazed lanterns, together with an armourer's forge, with bellows, which kept them blazing. Le Cocq lived in a hut nearby and it is hard to think of a more thankless task than his was. An improvement was effected in 1770, when oil lamps replaced the fires and more powerful lanterns succeeded them in 1790. By then, not surprisingly, Le Cocq had retired. In that year three towers were built, a most distinctive feature in lighthouse architecture. they were named, respectively, St Peter, St Thomas and Donjon. Possibly the last curious name was originally St John.

By then Trinity House was operating the Casquets in the same way as it controlled other lighthouses. Keepers were established, although it appears that only one was on duty at a time. He lived in a cottage — which survives — and a cutter brought him relief and supplies, which were augmented by produce grown in a small

Les Casquets Lighthouse in 1900.

garden, whose soil came from Alderney. Steps and paths cut in the rocks comprised two landing-places, situated on the north-east and south-west sides.

The entire building area was enclosed by a high and stout stone wall, still standing. All the materials needed for constructing lighthouses, cottage and wall had to be conveyed from Alderney and loading them onto the rock must have been both hazardous and difficult. The task was very well done and practically all the buildings to be seen today are original, although repairs and alterations take place from time to time.

In the middle of the last century the keeper was Lucas Houguez and he and his family (who shared his vigil on the rock) were visited by Mrs Lane Clarke in 1846, as she recorded in her guide book. Among other gifts she brought picture books for the children, who were amazed at illustrations of a cow and a donkey. It may well have been that some of the children had been born on the Casquets.

This was the family of whom a daughter became something of a literary figure, thanks to A. C. Swinburne's wonderful poem, 'Les Casquets', which tells of this unusual girl. She loved living there and when, one day, she was induced to visit relatives in Alderney, the experience horrified her. She declared it was too full of trouble and noise and, after a few days, she was only too glad to return to her lighthouse home. Nevertheless, later she fell in love with a man whom she met while he was working there and she married him. Her father, who seldom, if ever, seemed to have gone on leave, became paralysed and returned to Alderney on pension. He was succeeded by three keepers, a system in operation up to November, 1990, but their families did not share in their vigil.

In her book, Mrs Lane Clarke stated that there was a telegraph on the rock which enabled keepers to communicate with Alderney, over six miles away. The anonymous author of *Rambles among the Channel Islands* (published in about 1855), wrote that there were a warehouse and a shop on the Casquets. One presumes it was a workshop, for a more unlikely place for commerce would be hard to find. He wrote that the thick glass of the lighthouses was often broken by the sea and birds in stormy conditions.

In 1877 radical changes came about. The three lights were replaced by one, in the north-western tower, which was increased in height. In the eastern tower a fog signal was established and the eastern one became a store. Both were reduced in height. Since then the light's power has been greatly increased, a radio beacon enhances the value of the lighthouse, and in 1950 it was electrified. The old equipment, after 80 years' use, was removed by the Trinity vessel

Beacon. At about this time new lenses replaced those damaged by the R.A.F. during the war and the intensity of the light was increased to 2,830,000 candle power.

During the occupation the Germans used the light, but only when friendly ships needed it, and even then the power was reduced from that of pre-occupation days. Germans were stationed there and barbed wire was fixed to deter intruders. However, it did not prevent a visit by a British raiding party on the night of September 2, 1942. They came from Portland by motor torpedo boat and from her were transferred to the rock by an assault craft.

The twelve men took the 'garrison' by surprise and they offered no resistance. The seven Germans were found in bed and were taken off, still in pyjamas, by the invaders, who smashed the radio installation but spared the light and engine room. Although the raid was a success it did not deter the Germans from continuing to occupy the Casquets until May 17, 1945, when Trinity House took possession again.

A great change occurred in 1972, when a helicopter replaced the MFV *Burhou*, the lighthouse tender since 1946. A landing pad had been set on the eastern tower, but the boat still made occasional trips from Alderney. Her skipper, Nic Allen, who had served Trinity House as a pilot since 1929, died soon after making his last visit to the rock. Since 1972 helicopters have served the lighthouse, conveying keepers and their requirements to and fro, but heavier materials have been taken across those troubled waters by Trinity House ships, which also conveyed the Elder Brethren to the Casquets on their annual inspection of lighthouses in the Guernsey Bailiwick.

Early in 1990 storms damaged one of the paths and flights of steps, as well as the helicopter pad, most of which was washed away. This damage was repaired in the spring.

At the end of October, 1990, the lighthouse was changed from manual control to automatic, after many months of work to accomplish this. The automation involves a computer, two generators and a battery supply sufficient to provide power for five days, in the event of a total power failure. The foghorn has been renewed and is worked by firing a light beam northwards. When the beam encounters a fog bank it sets the horn operating.

St Thomas' tower houses the automatic system and the Donjon tower will no longer be in use and will be bricked up. The light itself is housed in St Peter's tower, together with the foghorn. The light, of 2,830,000 candle power, has a 28 miles circumference shining five times every half minute.

So, after 200 years, humanity has forsaken the Casquets and the rock has reverted to its original solitude. But man's ingenuity still dominates the rocks and this Channel sentinel will continue to aid the seafarer, even if it is now only a robot.

It is very unusual for a large book to be written about a single lighthouse, but this happened in 1972, when Rigby Graham's superb volume was published. Its name and subject was Les Casquets and it was limited to an edition of only thirty copies, costing £150 apiece. It abounded in drawings, photographs and much reading matter and the whole conception was a masterpiece of printing and binding — truly a collector's piece. The author also wrote another costly rarity: An Alderney Afternoon, which again included references to Les Casquets and some wrecks associated with these notorious rocks.

Alderney Lighthouse

This is the official name of that conspicuous building, but colloqually it is usually known as Mannez or Quesnard lighthouse, after these adjacent regions. In Eric Sharp's book, *Lighthouses of the Channel Islands*, he prefers to name it 'Quesnard'. It was built by William Baron, of Alderney, in 1912, doubtless because of the succession of wrecks nearby. It is 120 feet in height and its light and fog signal are powerful indeed. The signal and stores are in buildings beside the tower. The keepers have made life easier for Alderney folk by accepting emergency telephone calls and passing them on to the appropriate authorities.

In his book, *Alderney Fortress Island*, T. X. H. Pantcheff related that the Germans used the lighthouse as a navigational aid for night convoys. Otherwise it was out of action until Trinity House resumed control of it. Normally, the building is open to the public in the afternoon, provided the fog signal is not operating.

Alderney Lighthouse.

In *The Landscape of the Channel Islands*, Nigel Jee states that the lighthouse was built of brick. An examination of photographs taken when it was under construction does not bear this out. Granite is clearly visible, doubtless hewn from the nearby quarry. If brick was used, it must have been within the structure. Probably it was locally produced at the former brickfield on Le Grand Val, near the airport and perhaps this came into being when brick was used in certain parts of the forts. Brick is very evident in the former Coastguards' quarters at Longis and also in some residences in St Anne's.

While wrecks are abundant around Alderney, today they are far less numerous than in pre-lighthouse times, though they are almost bound to occur occasionally, as has been the case during the present century. Man cannot control the elements, though he may attempt to constrain them and, whether they are controlled by men or machines, these island lighthouses will continue to play their part in the maritime history of our shores for a very long time to come.

Ship Index
(Ships receiving only passing reference are omitted)

Alderney (bomb ketch) 34
Alderney (cargo ship) 34
Alderney (submarine) 33
Alderney (fishery protection vessel) 33, 34
Amethyst 22, 23
Armas 31
Arpha 10
Autocarrier 14

Behira 24
Brittany 14
Burhou 12
Burton 29

Carioca 24
Charles Ellison 29
Cimoni 23
Constantia S 31
Corrina 32
Courier 8, 9

Dasher 33
Devoniun 15

Edirne 30, 31
Emily Eveson 30
Empress 30
Experiment 5

Fawn 10
Felix de Absalo 28, 29
Forester's Future 17

Guernsey 10

Helper 10
Hope 5

Island Commodore 14
Isle of Alderney 34

Jupiter 23

Leros 28
Liverpool 25, 26
Louis Marchesi of Round Table 17
Lynn O'Dee 28

Marie Fanny 24
Mary & Victoria 17
Michael 19
Monarch 10

New Fawn 10

Patricia 11
Petit Raymond 26
Pioneer 18
Point Law 31
Portsea 26
Princess 7
Princess Royal 7

Queen of the Isles 7

Radford 14
Resolution 5
Rhenania 29, 30
Riduna 10

Serk 9
Staffa 13
Stella 24, 25

Vestal 11
Victory 19
Viper 25

White Heather 13

DEVON
DOG WALKS
WALKS ON & AROUND DARTMOOR

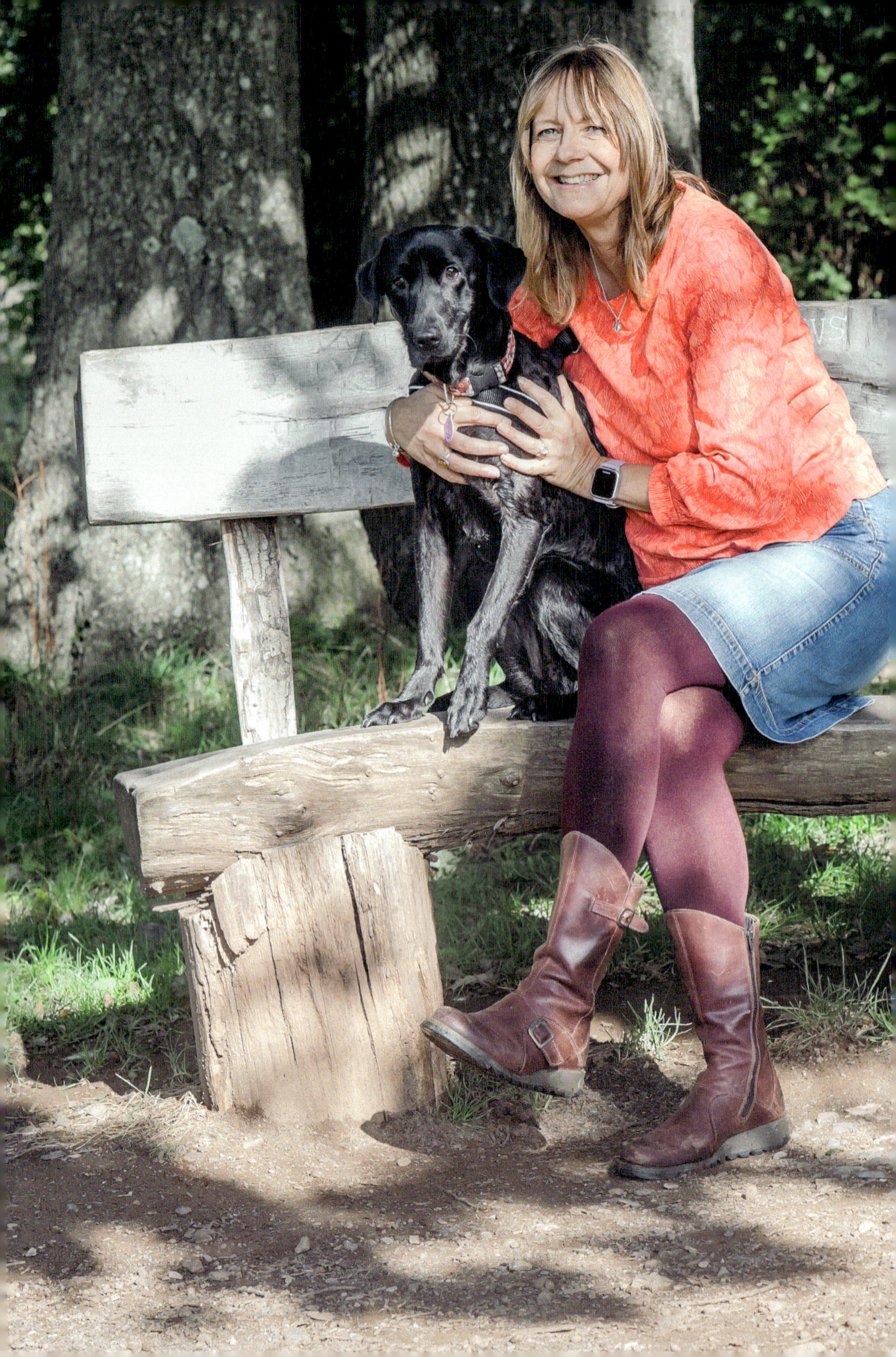

CONTENTS

Introduction
page 4

Enjoying Dartmoor Responsibly
page 5

● **WALK 01**
Chagford & the Two Moors Way
page 6

● **WALK 02**
Stone & Cairn Circles at Mardon Down
page 10

● **WALK 03**
Woods above Kennick Reservoir
page 14

● **WALK 04**
Lustleigh & the Bovey Valley
page 18

● **WALK 05**
Ilsington, Trumpeter & Haytor Vale
page 22

● **WALK 06**
Stover & the Sawdust Fusiliers
page 28

● **WALK 07**
Ramshorn Down
page 32

● **WALK 08**
Poundsgate & Spitchwick
page 36

● **WALK 09**
Manaton & Barrowman's Nose
page 40

● **WALK 10**
North Bovey & Easdon Tor
page 44

INTRODUCTION

When I was asked to write a book of dog walks, I thought long and hard about the sort of routes to include. I love to explore the moor, but I'm not a fan of the seven mile yomp across the wilderness, Ordinance Survey map fluttering in the wind. My ideal stroll would take in leafy lanes, a pretty village and almost certainly would have a viewpoint for the perfect picnic, or better still a pub or a tearoom for refreshments before or after! And so these walks (almost) all start and finish in a village, with either tantalising tor views or short forays amongst the heather and gorse, but never straying too far from civilisation.

These walks are all based on the east side of Dartmoor, in striking distance of Bovey Tracey, known locally as the 'Gateway to the Moor.'

For ease I have used the what3words app to give the most accurate start points and for tricky-to-find places. I really recommend downloading this and giving it a go – street addresses and postcodes aren't accurate enough to specify precise locations for rural areas. What3words has divided the world into 3 metre squares and given each square a unique combination of three words. Once you've loaded the code you'll be offered the choice of Google or Apple Maps to direct you to the specified location. It's magic!

My constant walking companion is my Labrador, Mo. Mo has been blind since birth and she was rejected by her mum as a pup and hand-reared. She and I became firm friends when at just two weeks old she was handed into the rescue centre where I worked. It wasn't long until I forgot all about my promise of not to bring my work home, and Mo became a permanent member of our family.

She and I like to walk for an hour or two every day, so these walks are all between 2 and 4.5 miles. I love to gawp at grand houses and Mo likes water, so most walks have a sprinkling of both.

I hope you enjoy the routes as much as Mo and I have enjoyed discovering them!

ENJOYING DARTMOOR RESPONSIBLY

Please park your car carefully – the little Dartmoor villages weren't built for traffic so please be considerate of locals and always ensure you leave room for farmers to carry out their work and for emergency vehicles to get through.

You are probably aware that the Dartmoor roads are very narrow and winding! If you are travelling in a motorhome Sat Nav might not be your friend, so check the best route for larger vehicles online before you set off: www.dartmoor.gov.uk/enjoy-dartmoor/planning-your-visit/travel-information

Please bag your dog's poo and take it home with you; don't leave bags lying around as animals will eat them or smaller wildlife will get stuck inside them. You can buy 'Love Moor Life' Dicky Bags from the National Park Visitor Centres (at Haytor, Postbridge or Princetown) for an easy odour-free way of carrying your dog's poop.

Follow the Dartmoor Ranger Code and ensure you keep your dogs on a lead:

🐾 during the lambing and ground nesting bird season (1st March – 31st July) – ground nesting birds, such as the skylark, meadow pipit and curlew can be scared away from their nest by a loose dog, meaning their eggs will get cold and the chicks die.

🐾 at all times when near or around livestock. A dog chasing livestock can cause a sheep, cow or pony great distress and a farmer can legally shoot a dog that is 'worrying' livestock.

🐾 during warm weather when there is a risk of adders in the undergrowth.

You can find more information about enjoying the moor with your dog here: www.dartmoor.gov.uk/enjoy-dartmoor/planning-your-visit/visiting-with-your-dog

Just in case you spot an animal in distress, the Livestock Protection Officer's number is 07873 587561.

WALK 01
CHAGFORD & THE TWO MOORS WAY

WHAT3WORDS:
NEWSREEL.TOWNHOUSE.MOTORING

DISTANCE:
Just over 2 miles

TIME:
It takes me about an hour

Chagford gets its name from the word *chag*, meaning gorse or broom, and *ford*, a shallow place where you cross a river. It's a lovely little town, based around an octagonal market house known as the Pepperpot, which was built in 1862. There are traditional thatched cottages, a 15th century church and many independent shops and eateries, making it a great place for a leisurely wander. Apparently, they even have a sunnier, drier climate than you will find on the western side of the moor!

6 | DOG WALKS IN DEVON

DOG WALKS IN DEVON | 7

WALKIES

Turn left out of the car park, towards the church and then carry straight on along Mill Street, passing the Three Crowns pub (which dates back to the 13th century and is reportedly haunted by the ghost of a cavalier poet who was killed there during the Civil War). Continue down the hill past the Spar shop until you reach a converted mill called Moorlands. Here fork right and walk down Mill Street, which is signposted to Gidleigh and Throwleigh. I enjoyed peeking up the driveways of some rather lovely houses as I walked along this road!

The road goes steeply downhill before you reach a crossroads with a big stone wall and the ruins of an old mill in front of you. Turn right and you will cross the River Teign over a lovely old bridge which dates back to the 16th century. Take the footpath on the right immediately after the bridge, going through a five-bar gate with a 'Fishing by Permit only' sign. Walk along the path and through the kissing gate onto the Two Moors Way. Follow the path and you will see several huge, ancient trees with granite walls built around their bases for protection. Go through a wooden gate with a footpath sign on it, following the river and ignoring a footpath to the left.

Continue past a lovely old converted mill on the other side of the river.

Walk along the river, through several fields and gates, enjoying the views of the rolling hills on your left. After a little wooden gate you will reach a weir, with rope swings evidence of sunny summer afternoon swims. Continue on to a stile, crossing a couple more fields until you reach a wooden bridge with a signpost to Rushford Bridge. Cross here then bear slightly left across the field to a hole in the hedge, following a well-trodden path to join the road at the lovely old Rushford Bridge. Turn right to walk uphill to Chagford. When you reach the T-junction turn right, and walk back up to Chagford's main square, passing the school and the fire station as you go.

SPECIAL INTEREST

YOU MAY BE LUCKY ENOUGH TO SEE THE FLASH OF TURQUOISE AS A KINGFISHER SWOOPS BY. DIPPERS ENJOY THE FAST-MOVING WATER AND GREY WAGTAILS WITH THEIR GREY AND YELLOW PLUMAGE CAN BE SPOTTED ALL ALONG THE RIVER. OTTERS HAVE BEEN SEEN FURTHER ALONG THE RIVER TEIGN, SO KEEP YOUR EYES PEELED!

USEFUL
Information

START: Chagford Health Centre car park, near the church.

WHAT3WORDS: newsreel.townhouse.motoring

TERRAIN: A stroll through the town to start, and then a lovely flat river walk which takes you along a short section of the Two Moors Way. The Two Moors Way covers 102 miles from Ivybridge in Dartmoor to Lynmouth in Exmoor. You will be relieved to know that this is just a short section, down leafy lanes, across fields and along the River Teign, with a fairly gentle return uphill at the end of the walk.

PARKING: Chagford Health Centre car park TQ13 8BW – charges apply.

REFRESHMENTS: Plenty of choice in Chagford! Dog friendly tea rooms and pubs and a supermarket to grab picnic goodies.

TOILETS: The toilets are in the octagonal building in the Market Square and are one of the few public loos that I've visited with a dressing table and a vase of flowers!

DOG BINS: You will find dog bins in the town centre.

02

WALK 02
STONE & CAIRN CIRCLES AT MARDON DOWN

WHAT3WORDS:
BADMINTON.ENFORCED.TRIO

DISTANCE:
Either just under 2 miles or just under 1 mile

TIME:
It takes me just over an hour to walk the 2 miles at a stomp, but allow longer to explore the stone circles and enjoy the sweeping views

This is a fabulous walk for blowing away the cobwebs! Although it's short (with an even shorter version possible) you'll feel like you've been immersed in Dartmoor's historic landscape. With breathtaking views (don't forget your binoculars) and ancient stone circles, this delightful route will give you a good dose of Dartmoor fresh air!

MARDON DOWN
Headless Cross

Cairn Circle

Stacombe

START

10 | DOG WALKS IN DEVON

DOG WALKS IN DEVON | 11

WALKIES

From the car park walk along the distinct track that goes straight up the hill towards the skyline, immediately taking the left-hand fork which climbs towards the brow of the hill. Just before the top you reach a wide track where you turn left and then immediately right, stepping into the remains of one of the biggest stone circles on Dartmoor.

Thirty-eight metres in diameter and hailing from the Bronze Age, this was probably a ceremonial site. Very little of it remains now, but from here you will have the most amazing views from Haytor to the left, Cosdon Hill to the right and Hound Tor, Hamel Down, Fernworthy Forest, Hangingstone Hill, High Willhays and Yes Tor in-between!

Continue on your way, taking the path by the large stone that sticks out at a very funny angle! Watch out for a wind farm away in the distance to guide your way. You pass the remains of a smaller stone circle on your left, before joining the original track, where you turn left. Enjoy the far-reaching views as you meander along, ignoring any forks to the left and right and keeping the windmills in sight. After a while the path drops down the hill and you will come to a beautiful cairn circle on your left. (What3words: pizzas.frostbite.playroom)

After you've stopped to admire the stones and take photos, carry on downhill on the grassy track.

For the short loop – take the first track to the right, going straight over where the paths cross, and wandering back to the car park.

For the longer walk, with a fantastic 360° view of Devon, carry on down the hill to a single standing stone (known as the Headless Cross) and cross the road, walking over a gravel parking area and then straight ahead up a really wide grassy track. As you near the top of the hill you will have a glorious view across to North Devon – you may even be able to see the huge satellite dish at Bude if it's a clear day.

After a lone conifer tree you will reach a crossroads, just as you start to go downhill. Take the right-hand path and wander between the ferns and gorse. Look out for the white glow of Haldon Belvedere, a castle built as a memorial in 1788, which always seems to be shining whatever the weather!

Turn right again when you reach the next grassy path, and you will see Blackingstone Rock a few miles away. It's one of the highest tors on Dartmoor at 24 metres from its base to the top and it has a terrifying metal ladder for people to climb! Follow the well-defined track as it swoops around the top of the hill in a wide loop, giving you gorgeous views in each direction. Soon you will be facing the wind farm again, and having come full circle, you'll arrive back at the wide track you walked up, turning left to head back down to the road.

Walk across the road again by the Headless Cross and head back up the grassy slope, taking the first fork on the left. When you reach the crossroads turn left and if you ignore any turnings off this track you will soon be back at your car.

USEFUL
Information

START: This walk starts out on the moor near Smallridge, close to Moretonhampstead. The best way to find the start is to use what3words to guide you.

WHAT3WORDS: badminton.enforced.trio

TERRAIN: This is a fairly easy walk along springy grassy tracks, with reasonably gentle inclines. It is a high part of the moor and it can be windy up there – don't forget your hat!

PARKING: Use what3words: badminton.enforced.trio to take you to a gravel parking area surrounded by boulders, in the shade of a tree.

REFRESHMENTS: No refreshments on this route, but Moretonhampstead is just 4 miles away, with a whole wealth of amenities.

TOILETS: None on the route, the nearest are in Moretonhampstead or in the car park at nearby Trenchford Reservoir (what3words: toasted.ordeals.prefer)

DOG BINS: None on this route – it's just wild moor up here!

SPECIAL INTEREST

COMMON PLANTS INCLUDE GORSE, HEATHER AND BILBERRY. FAIRY RINGS AND MANY VARIETIES OF FUNGI CAN BE FOUND IN AUTUMN. IN SPRING AND SUMMER YOU WILL HEAR THE GLORIOUS SOUND OF SKYLARKS SINGING; OTHER BIRDS INCLUDE THE STONECHAT AND MEADOW PIP. IN THE SUMMER LOOK OUT FOR ADDERS AND THE RARE HIGH BROWN FRITILLARY BUTTERFLY WHICH LIVES IN THE BRACKEN. YOU ARE LIKELY TO SEE PONIES AND COWS MEANDERING ALONG THIS STRETCH OF THE MOOR.

03

WALK 03
WOODS ABOVE KENNICK RESERVOIR

WHAT3WORDS:
SQUASHES.IRONY.EMERALDS

DISTANCE:
Approximately 3.5 miles

TIME:
It takes me about an hour and 15 minutes

Kennick, Tottiford and Trenchford form part of the South West Lakes Trust. There are some lovely walks around the banks of Trenchford and Tottiford Reservoirs, but they do get quite busy, and you're asked to keep your dog on a lead and out of the water... not easy if you have a boisterous labrador! Kennick Reservoir is restricted to anglers only, due to its narrow banks, but this walk takes you up into the woods above, giving you gorgeous views down to the lake, with lots of places where your dog can run free.

14 | DOG WALKS IN DEVON

SPECIAL INTEREST

KENNICK IS THE LARGEST OF THE THREE NEIGHBOURING RESERVOIRS WHICH SUPPLY TORBAY WITH DRINKING WATER. CONSTRUCTED IN 1861, TOTTIFORD IS THE OLDEST RESERVOIR ON DARTMOOR, FOLLOWED BY KENNICK IN 1881 AND TRENCHFORD IN 1903. THEY HAVE A COMBINED CAPACITY OF 2,011 MEGALITRES WHEN FULL.

THE WALK STARTS ON THE ROAD BETWEEN KENNICK AND TOTTIFORD RESERVOIRS, WITH GLORIOUS VIEWS ACROSS BOTH LAKES AND THE CHANCE TO SEE GEESE, COOT, MALLARDS AND HERONS. I HAVE ALSO SEEN A KINGFISHER HERE! AS YOU MAKE YOUR WAY THROUGH LAPLOYD PLANTATION YOU MAY SEE DEER, BUZZARDS AND BUTTERFLIES INCLUDING PEACOCKS, PAINTED LADIES, TORTOISESHELLS AND MEADOW BLUES. THERE ARE LOVELY SPRING FLOWERS, INCLUDING BLUEBELLS AND IN EARLY SUMMER BEAUTIFUL PINK RHODODENDRON. BUT THE REAL STAR OF THE SHOW IS THE GORSE WHICH IS PROLIFIC AROUND HERE AND FILLS THE AIR WITH ITS COCONUT SCENT!

WALKIES

Starting by Kennick Trout Fishery's Permit Office, walk past the reservoirs and as you climb uphill take the footpath to the left which is well signed and takes you along a pine-needly path. Stay on this track, ignoring turnings off, until you reach an open stony clearing, where you turn left to stay on a gravelly path around the edge of a fir tree wood. You will reach a junction with a Quaker Burial Ground marker stone on the wall in front – Quakers lived here in the late 17th-mid-18th century and met at the nearby farmhouse. It's thought that about twenty people were buried in a Quaker burial ground in a nearby field.

Turn right and walk along until you reach a white house called Beacon Farm. Take the path to the left which is signposted 'Bridleway to Laployd Rides'. Walk up the hill, listening to the tall trees whooshing in the wind, and at the end of the treeline carry straight on up a narrow path between two fields. There are lovely views towards Exeter to the right, and deer often graze here. However, it can be quite muddy!

Walk up the hill, ignoring a right-hand turning to Bridford and continuing straight ahead, disregarding a further right-hand path into the wood. Instead stay in the sun around the edge of the trees, following the path all the way to the top of the hill; ignore the rabbity paths which go off either side and keep walking until the path enters the wood and becomes stony. Turn left at the junction signposted Smithacott (a small hamlet whose name means Cottage of the Smiths).

Take this path down the hill, enjoying glimpses of the reservoir on your left through the trees, and at the bottom turn left signposted Clampitt Cottage. This is my favourite part; in spring the gorse bushes shine bright yellow on either side of the path and smell delicious! On hot July days, once the yellow has faded, you can hear faint popping noises as the seed pods burst open – one of my favourite sounds of summer! There are lots of Christmas trees growing here, with the reservoir glistening in the sun behind them. Look out for butterflies, attracted to the gorse, and shiny oil beetles that may be slowly crossing the path at your feet. Cross a trickle of a stream and as the path becomes wider, climb up-hill. Pop your dog on a lead for this section if they are prone to explore, as there are stock in the fields to the right of the path ahead and some gateways that they might be able to crawl under. You may be lucky enough to see free-range piglets scampering around, and as you continue on the path, you'll see the remains of Clampitt Farm, which dates back to the 14th century, on your left.

You will soon find yourself back at the junction with the Quaker Burial Ground marker stone; a section which may be wet and muddy. Take the right-hand fork and retrace your steps, turning right at the end of the track before heading straight down the pine-needly path back to the beginning, signposted Kennick Reservoir.

USEFUL
Information

START: The road between Kennick and Tottiford Reservoirs, near the Trout Fishery. The postcode for this road is EX6 7NZ but being in the middle of nowhere it won't take you directly to the Fishery's Permit Office where the walk starts. The best way to find the exact starting point is to use what3words.

WHAT3WORDS: squashes.irony.emeralds

TERRAIN: Easy-going woodland tracks, fairly gentle inclines. Can be wet and muddy in places.

PARKING: There is a small parking area near Kennick Trout Fishery's Permit Office and more parking on the right-hand side of the road just past the lakes, opposite the footpath into the wood.

REFRESHMENTS: None on the route, although there is sometimes a food van at Trenchford Reservoir car park (what3words: toasted.ordeals. prefer). Bovey Tracey and Moretonhampstead are both nearby and have a wealth of lovely places to eat.

TOILETS: In the car park at nearby Trenchford Reservoir (what3words: toasted.ordeals.prefer).

DOG BINS: None on this route.

DOG WALKS IN DEVON | 17

04

WALK 04
LUSTLEIGH & THE BOVEY VALLEY

WHAT3WORDS:
MEMBER.GALLOPING.DWELL

DISTANCE:
Approximately 4 miles

TIME:
It takes me about 1 hour and 45 minutes

A hilly and quite challenging walk, but worth the effort for the beautiful woodland paths, a bubbling river in a beautiful valley and a medieval packhorse bridge on the route. You end with a village stroll past beautiful thatched cottages with pretty gardens.

18 | DOG WALKS IN DEVON

USEFUL
Information

START: Lustleigh Village, near the church TQ13 9TA.

WHAT3WORDS: member.galloping.dwell

TERRAIN: Rough, uneven woodland paths and riverbanks that can be muddy. Quiet lanes and steep hills.

PARKING: Park carefully in the village. There is limited parking so avoid busy times if you can.

REFRESHMENTS: The Dairy is a lovely community-owned village shop, open 7 days a week (until 1pm on Sundays) and perfect for picking up a picnic or a snack to keep you going en route. Primrose Tea Rooms, which is open seasonally, offers light lunches, cakes and cream teas. Or you could try The Cleave restaurant and bar, a 15th Century Inn which welcomes dogs in the bar and the beer garden.

TOILETS: Public loos just before the orchard.

DOG BINS: In the village.

WALKIES

Start in the centre of the village and walk down between the Dairy and a house called the Old Post Office (it's well worth stopping at the Dairy for a warm pasty, I can highly recommend the roasted vegetable!). Go into the community orchard, formally used to grow cider apples and gifted to the village in 1966. This is particularly beautiful in spring when the fruit trees are flowering. Walk through the orchard, stopping to admire the huge granite rock in the middle. The throne on top is where the village May Queen is crowned each year and the names of previous queens are carved into the stone. To qualify to be May Queen candidates must have danced around the May Pole on at least five occasions!

Cross the little wooden bridge leading out of the orchard and through the gate walking straight on uphill on a little muddy path. At the junction carry straight on to the lane where you turn left and then right up a little footpath through the woods, keeping the fence on your right and ignoring the path signposted to your left, until you pop out onto a lane near a house called Kemerton. Proceed up a very steep hill to a lovely hamlet called Pethybridge. Stop to appreciate the view back down to the village on the way up!

Pass between two thatched cottages to a T-junction where you turn left, to reach a further junction opposite a house called Cleavelands St Mary where you turn right. Shortly afterwards, just before Wray Cottage, turn left up a stony track. You may have to look closely for this – at the time of writing the signpost to 'Lustleigh Cleave' is broken and easy to miss! Walk uphill to the Cleave (an Old English word meaning cliff), passing through the charmingly named 'Heaven's Gate' into a Special Area of Conservation.

Walk a short way downhill into the valley and then turn left to go through a wooden gate into Hisley Wood, signposted Hisley Bridge and part of the East Dartmoor National Nature Reserve. Stay on this path, which twists and turns in the shadow of the high moor, all the way down to the bottom of the hill. As you walk you will start to hear the rushing water of the River Bovey in the valley below, and you should get glimpses of the bubbling white water through the trees. Keep walking downhill, ignoring paths off, until you reach the river at a beautiful old packhorse bridge which was originally for farmers travelling between Manaton and Lustleigh.

Don't go across the bridge, or take the wide track, but instead walk along the riverbank, with the river on your right. Pass (or stop and admire the tranquil view) at a little bench overlooking the river. Go through a gate signed East Dartmoor National Nature Reserve. Walk along the riverbank, looking out for the ponies that are often brought in to graze this section. You may notice some bat boxes, looking a little like upside down bird houses, which are part of a project studying the Barbastelle Bat, a species rarely found in Europe but thriving in the Bovey Valley. Follow the water to a wide green clearing and continue to follow the path keeping the river on your right. You leave the nature reserve through a gate into a field, often occupied by grazing sheep. Walk across the field to a metal gate and go through onto a quiet lane, turning left to go up a very steep hill. You may start to feel your calves at this point!

Take the first lane right and follow it downhill. As the path widens turn right to continue downwards, and then right at a fork where you can just about read the words 'Wreyland' on a weathered signpost. You'll pass through the remains of an old railway bridge before forking right again. Walk down this leafy track to the water. Stay on the path, with a fence on your left, until you come to Wray Brook which you cross via a wooden bridge (there were lots of snowdrops along this route when I walked it in February). Turn left and look out for the remains of an old railway viaduct across the stream. The path forks at the end; take the right-hand track, following footpath signs up big steps along the edge of a field. At the very top, leave the field via the wooden gate onto a tarmac drive by a house called 'Lindale'.

Turn left, following the drive downhill towards a thatched cottage and at the junction with the road turn left and then left again to enjoy a meandering path lined with beautiful thatched cottages; including Wreyland Manor, which dates back to the 16th Century and has its own cricket pitch! Go under a railway bridge and back into Lustleigh, noting the stone cross on the village green which was erected in memory of Henry Tudor, Rector 1888-1904.

SPECIAL INTEREST

ONE OF THE MOST PICTURESQUE VILLAGES IN DEVON, LUSTLEIGH IS SURROUNDED BY FIELDS, MEADOWS AND WOODS. BIRDWATCHERS MIGHT BE LUCKY ENOUGH TO SEE SPARROWHAWKS, KINGFISHERS AND DIPPERS. THIS VALLEY IS PARTICULARLY WELL KNOWN FOR ITS BUTTERFLIES, AND KEEN SPOTTERS MAY SEE THE SPECKLED WOOD, MEADOW, BRIMSTONE, COMMA AND INTRIGUINGLY NAMED GREEN HAIRSTREAK BUTTERFLIES!

05

WALK 05
ILSINGTON, TRUMPETER & HAYTOR VALE

WHAT3WORDS:
WINEMAKER.ANNOUNCE.GRADES

DISTANCE:
Approximately 4.5 miles

TIME:
Allow 2.5 hours

A lovely walk which includes all my favourite things – interesting houses, cool woodland streams, a short stretch of open moor, village paths with hedgerows full of honeysuckle and a couple of refreshment stops!

22 | DOG WALKS IN DEVON

USEFUL
Information

START: The Church Lychgate, next to The Old Post Office, Ilsington TQ13 9RL.

WHAT3WORDS: winemaker.announce.grades

TERRAIN: Quiet country lanes, some steep climbs, stony tracks and moorland.

PARKING: Unrestricted on-road parking in the village (try to avoid school drop off and pick up times).

REFRESHMENTS: The Carpenters Arms, Ilsington, The Rock Inn, Haytor Vale. There is an award-winning community-run village store in Ilsington, just past the pub.

TOILETS: In the pubs, but for customers only. There is a visitor's centre at Haytor with public toilets a 5 minute drive from Ilsington TQ13 9XT.

DOG BINS: None on the route, but there is a bin near The Carpenters Arms in Ilsington Village.

DOG WALKS IN DEVON | 23

WALKIES

Start the walk from the church's lychgate, next to The Old Post Office. The lychgate has an unusual little room above the gateway, which used to house a school until 1639, when it collapsed with a teacher and seventeen schoolchildren inside. Happily, no one was seriously hurt, and the room was later rebuilt.

Set off uphill and turn left at the T-junction onto the main road out of Ilsington, heading westwards towards Haytor. You will pass houses called Kufena and Stoneycombe and then the vicarage and the cemetery on your left. Shortly afterwards turn right, signposted Trumpeter. This is a lovely quiet lane with great views and glimpses of Saddle Tor. There is also a gorgeous little stall selling flowers and home-grown vegetables which you may want to return to!

Keep going through the little hamlet of Trumpeter, past the houses, until you see a Public Footpath sign on the left, pointing the way to the Moor and Haytor Vale.

Passing Smallacombe Farm, cross a trickle of a stream and bear left, through a wooden gate, then immediately follow the path to the right which is signposted 'To the Moor'. Climb quite steeply along a stony track. Don't forget to stop and look at the view occasionally – you can see over the valley back to Ilsington church.

At the top, turn left at Shotts House, onto a lane which takes you past some beautiful houses. In fact, this stretch used to be called 'Millionaires' Row' at the start of the twentieth century, when several wealthy people lived or visited here, including philanthropists Dame Violet Wills, her sister Ella Rowcroft (who founded the local hospice), and the suffragette, Christabel Pankhurst.

There are some wonderful viewpoints here – which Dame Violet saved for future generations by forbidding any electric pylons to be built above ground! You can see across rolling hills and patchwork countryside all the way to the sea at Teignmouth. This section is particularly beautiful during the rhododendron season in late spring.

Keep going to the end of the lane, which opens up into a gravelled turning point, and go through the turnstile into woodland. Straight ahead you will see the entrance to an old iron ore mine, which in its heyday would have employed 80 people. From here, turn right, heading up hill, following a bridlepath sign to Haytor Vale. Follow this little path to the top, where you turn left onto the road and then left again to pass a row of cottages which were built in 1826 to house quarry workers.

Continue past the Rock Inn (or stop for a quick drink in their lovely garden!) until you reach the T-junction at a bungalow called Widdecombe's Rest. Turn left and go down the hill, passing a sign to Pinchaford and going past a small garage. There are glimpses of Saddle Tor and Bagtor Down to the right.

When you get to the next junction (called Smokey Cross) turn sharp right, almost back on yourself, following a small track with a bridle path sign. You will soon go past a small artist's studio with a painted boat outside. Follow the lane up the hill to a gate. Go through the gate which leads onto the moor at the foot of Bagtor Down and turn left. There are lots of different rabbity tracks amongst the gorse; it doesn't matter which one you take as long as you keep the wall on your left. The bracken can be quite overgrown close to the wall, so try to keep to the slightly higher well-trodden path. It's a good idea to keep dogs on a lead in this section as you may suddenly come upon grazing sheep or cows.

After approximately a quarter of a mile you turn left downhill onto a bridle path marked 'The Dartmoor Way'. If you have the what3words app you are looking for noon.stood.highways.

The next section can be quite tricky; it's steep and uneven with loose stones underfoot. This goes all the way down to a pretty section of the River Lemon, which you cross via a small clapper bridge.

Climb the path up to the road, and at the top turn right and continue to the crossroads, signed Birchanger Cross, where you turn left and walk along a small country lane with high hedges either side. Pass an old Methodist church which has been converted into a house immediately bearing left at the junction onto Honeywell Lane. Stay on this lane all the way back to the village, passing Portland Villa on the right and a children's playground on your left. This road leads straight back into Ilsington, where it ends at a T-junction, with the church to the left and the pub to the right.

SPECIAL INTEREST

WILDLIFE MAY INCLUDE THE SPECTACULAR EMPEROR MOTH, RARE FRITILLARY BUTTERFLIES (WHOSE CATERPILLARS FEED ON THE VIOLETS PEEPING FROM UNDER THE BRACKEN) AND YOU MAY SEE AND HEAR BUZZARDS OVERHEAD.

DEVON
DOG WALKS

- **WALK 01**
  Chagford & the Two Moors Way
  newsreel.townhouse.motoring   *page 6*
- **WALK 02**
  Stone & Cairn Circles at Mardon Down
  badminton.enforced.trio   *page 10*
- **WALK 03**
  Woods above Kennick Reservoir
  squashes.irony.emeralds   *page 14*
- **WALK 04**
  Lustleigh & the Bovey Valley
  member.galloping.dwell   *page 18*
- **WALK 05**
  Ilsington, Trumpeter & Haytor Vale
  winemaker.announce.grades   *page 22*
- **WALK 06**
  Stover & the Sawdust Fusiliers
  tucked.distract.lads   *page 28*
- **WALK 07**
  Ramshorn Down
  rounds.belly.sprouting   *page 32*
- **WALK 08**
  Poundsgate & Spitchwick
  cutaway.mainframe.echo   *page 36*
- **WALK 09**
  Manaton & Barrowman's Nose
  responses.outbid.implanted   *page 40*
- **WALK 10**
  North Bovey & Easdon Tor
  mediate.strumming.blotchy   *page 44*

Sourton

Gunnislake

Tamar Valley Area of Outstanding Natural Beauty

Woolwell

Saltash

PLYMOUTH

Dartmoor National Park

EXETER

Okehampton · Whidden Down · Chagford · Moretonhampstead · Topsham

01 · 02 · 03 · 04 · 05 · 06 · 07 · 08 · 09 · 10

Widecombe in the Moor · Dartmeet · Bovey Tracey · Kingsteignton · Newton Abbot · Dawlish · Teignmouth

Ashburton · Buckfastleigh

TORQUAY

Dartington · Totnes · Paignton · Brixham

South Brent · Ivybridge · Dartmouth

South Devon Area of Outstanding Natural Beauty

Hope Cove · Salcombe

06

WALK 06
STOVER & THE SAWDUST FUSILIERS

WHAT3WORDS:
TUCKED.DISTRACT.LADS

DISTANCE:
Approximately 4.5 miles

TIME:
Allow a little over 2 hours

This isn't exactly a moor walk, but it is just a stone's throw from Bovey Tracey and, unusually for these parts, is a lovely flat route. There is a delightful walk around the lake, but dogs must be on a lead. I'd been doing that walk for years without realising there was a much longer route where dogs can run free and you can get away from the crowds!

SPECIAL INTEREST

STOVER COUNTRY PARK FORMED PART OF THE 80,000-ACRE ESTATE ACQUIRED BY JAMES TEMPLER, A DEVONIAN ENTREPRENEUR, IN THE LATE EIGHTEENTH CENTURY. HE ALSO BUILT THE STOVER CANAL, WHICH WE SEE LATER IN THE WALK AT VENTIFORD, AND THE HAYTOR GRANITE TRAMWAY WHICH FORMS MUCH OF THE TEMPLER WAY WHICH YOU WILL SEE SIGNPOSTED ALONG THIS ROUTE. STOVER LAKE IS HOME TO A WEALTH OF WATER BIRDS BUT IS A SITE OF SPECIAL SCIENTIFIC INTEREST PRIMARILY BECAUSE OF THE DRAGONFLY POPULATION - 19 SPECIES HAVE BEEN RECORDED HERE INCLUDING THE WONDERFULLY NAMED HAIRY DRAGONFLY!

USEFUL
Information

START: Stover Country Park TQ12 6QG.

WHAT3WORDS: tucked.distract.lads

TERRAIN: Lakeside paths, muddy fields, woodland and village lanes. Can be boggy and puddly in wet weather so wear walking boots or wellingtons.

PARKING: The entrance to the park is on the A382 Bovey Tracey to Newton Abbot road near Trago Mills. There is a parking fee of £3.50 to park for the whole day, which will enable you to take your time, enjoy the wildlife and maybe stop for tea and cake along the way!

REFRESHMENTS: There is usually an ice cream/coffee van at Stover Country Park. Halfway round the walk you'll find the Locks Bridge Tea Garden, which is open Wednesday to Sunday, 10am until 3pm. I highly recommend a cup of tea and a slice of lemon cake to keep you going!

TOILETS: At Stover Country Park and at the Locks Bridge Tea Garden (for customers).

DOG BINS: Several around the lake.

WALKIES

Start the walk at the Visitor Centre and make your way to the lake, turning right when you reach the water (dogs must be kept on the lead for this section but can be allowed to run free once we move away from the Country Park). After passing a bird hide on your left, walk across a wooden slatted bridge/pontoon to continue round the lake. You will pass an aerial walkway (it's well worth taking this short detour to look at the birds on the feeder and the squirrels scurrying around underneath, looking for dropped food!) and then continue to the crossroads. Look for the turning on the right, signposted 'WW1 Canadian Forestry Corps Sculpture'.

Follow this track, taking a bridge over a stream (passing a beach area with the Ted Hughes Poetry Post with the poem 'Roe Deer' on your left). Carry on through a wooden gate, along a section which can become a bit puddly (to say the least) in wet weather. Cross an old cobblestone bridge until the track forks left and you may see the Canadian flag fluttering in the wind. Follow the track, passing the rear entrance to Stover School which was once the main home of the Templer family. You will soon see an unusual war memorial to 'The Sawdust Fusiliers'; these carved wooden figures of two men and a horse commemorate the Canadian soldiers who came to Devon during the First World War and produced timber which was sent to battlefields in France and Belgium where it was used for building trenches, roads, railways and huts.

After admiring the statues, keep going, ignoring any turnings until on your right you see a big yellow 'Safety Starts Here' sign at the entrance to Imery's Quarry. Immediately to your left is a footpath signposted the 'Heritage Trail', which you take, continuing across the fields to the road. Enjoy the views of Teigngrace Church – a Georgian building designed in a style known as 'Strawberry Hill Gothic'. Originally the church was part of Stover estate, serving the village and its estate and canal workers.

Dogs should be on a lead if there are cattle in the field and keep them close before the kissing gate to ensure they're safe from traffic. At the road turn right and walk until you reach a left hand turning signed 'public footpath' and 'Heritage Trail'. This takes you down a private road to Teign Manor and The Barns. It looks as if you're walking into someone's private drive, but it's a well-trodden footpath so don't worry!

At the end of the drive, you cross through two metal gates over a disused railway track (where in 1983 Prince

Charles and Princess Diana spent a night on the Royal Train!). You arrive at the Locks Bridge Tea Garden and if you time it right this makes a good pit-stop!

Cross the bridge in front of the café, then turn left, ignoring signs to the Heritage Trail for now, and instead take the Templer Way. After a while the road forks and you go left signposted 'Ventiford Basin, pedestrians only'. Make your way along this pleasant path over a little wooden footbridge to the canal basin. Years ago, clay from the local area was brought here, loaded onto barges and taken down to the River Teign where it was transferred to ships at the docks in Teignmouth. In 1820, a Granite Tramway came here from the quarries at Haytor to enable Dartmoor granite to follow the same route as the clay. This Dartmoor granite was used in the construction of many prominent buildings in London.

Walk to the end of the canal basin, pop your dog on a lead and turn left to go under the railway bridge and then turn right onto the road. Ignore the turning on your right, signposted Stover Bike Route, and walk along the road, watching out for bikes and cars along this section. Pass Swallow Cottage and Lavender Cottage, which has a little fruit and plant sale next to the road. Ignore the next turning right into Summer Lane but look out shortly afterwards for a footpath on your left, signposted 'Heritage Trail' which takes you through a kissing gate and back into Stover Woods. Your aim now is to find your way back to the lake, and the easiest way is to keep as close to the fence on your left as you can, following a windy, uneven path with lots of roots and obstacles – so walk with care! Cross over a small wooden bridge, ignore any signs now for the heritage trail going right, and keep left at any forks.

Continue over a larger wooden bridge, taking the left track and walking alongside the babbling stream, keeping it close and on your left. If you stay with the stream, it will take you all the way back to the bridge we crossed earlier with the 'Roe Deer' poem. Once you reach that point turn right and make your way back to the lake. This time, go straight on at the junction and cross the bridge, turning left and walking in an anti-clockwise direction around the lake and back across another bridge to the Visitor Centre where we started.

DOG WALKS IN DEVON | 31

WALK 07
RAMSHORN DOWN

WHAT3WORDS:
ROUNDS.BELLY.SPROUTING

DISTANCE:
4.5 miles

TIME:
It takes me just over an hour and 30 minutes

I love a walk with a view and an interesting feature, so this walk ticks both boxes! Although it's a circular walk there is a section where you walk up to Ramshorn Down and then retrace your steps down to return to the main walk. It is well worth the climb up for the view. The local parish council has marked the summit area with a stone, mapping out the view and putting a ring of standing stones around it.

SPECIAL INTEREST

THE VIEWS FROM RAMSHORN DOWN ARE FABULOUS. THE WALK THROUGH THE QUIET RORA WOODS MAY GIVE YOU A GLIMPSE OF A DEER, AND YOU WILL DEFINITELY SEE BLUEBELLS IN LATE SPRING. IN THE AUTUMN THE TREES - ENGLISH OAK, BIRCHES, ROWAN, HAZEL AND HOLLY - GIVE A FABULOUS DISPLAY OF COLOUR.

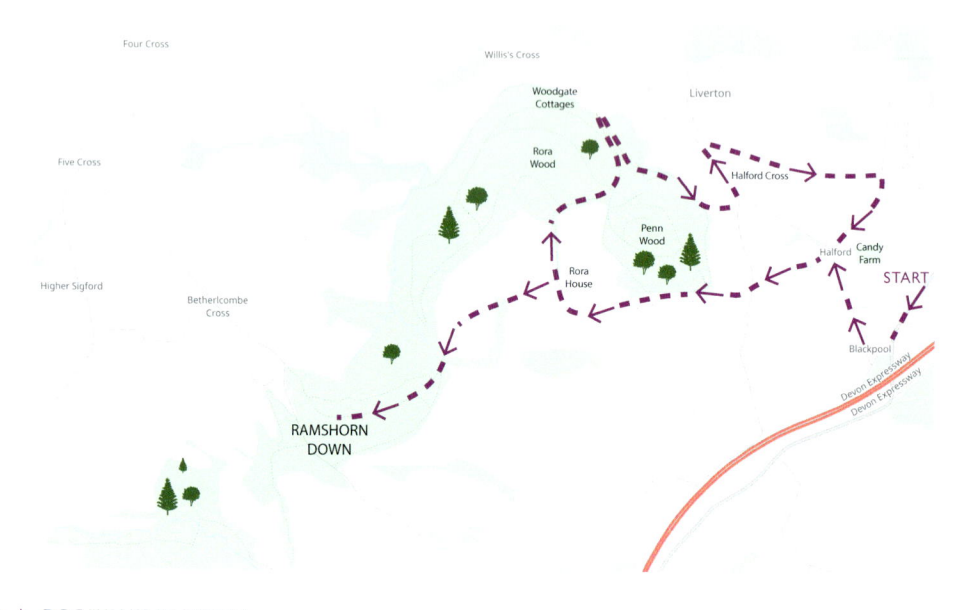

DOG WALKS IN DEVON | 33

WALKIES

Follow the pavement up the hill and take the first road on the right, which passes Blackpool School and meanders down the road, between Candy Cottage and Candy Farm. Turn left at the junction just before a pretty row of houses called Leat Cottages and then go immediately left over a stile into a field. It can be muddy! Dogs can have a run along here as the path, which takes you through two fields, is fenced off. When you reach the stile at the end, cross the road and walk down the drive of Rora House, following a public footpath sign. Rora House in now a Christian Fellowship meeting place, so if you walk up on a Sunday morning you may encounter a few cars, but it's quite a rough, pot holey track so hopefully no one will be driving too fast!

Keep on the lane, passing their big green information sign, and continuing past the lovely pink manor house which dates back to 1885. Keeping your dog on a lead, carry on up the path which goes between two stone walls to a wooden gate (with footpath signs) and enter the courtyard of Rora Farmhouse. Turn right up the hill, with the gorgeous, thatched farmhouse on your left and stables on your right, heading for a gate and footpath sign at the top of the hill. Go through the gate and take the left-hand footpath up the hill. Keep climbing, taking the left path at a fork, which has a footpath sign, and stay on this well-trodden path straight on through the field and between two bramble hedges. The path opens up into a field at the top – stop and catch your breath as you take in the glorious views across the treetops. The sea at Teignmouth is visible in the distance, and there are lovely glimpses of Haytor on your right and Belvedere Castle at Haldon behind you. Follow the path to the top of the field, turn left when you reach the track and head up towards the metal gate. Go through the kissing gate at its side and carry on right up to the top of the hill, following the footpath sign and ignoring a fork off to the left.

The main path becomes wide and clear, flanked by gorse bushes, and at the brow of the hill you will see a modern stone circle with a marked stone, laid by the parish council in 2020. This stone points out the incredible 360° views across the moor to Teignmouth, Plymouth, Torbay and Okehampton respectively.

Now retrace your steps, back down the hill, through the kissing gate and down through the fields – enjoying the views again on the way down. You will eventually find yourself back at the gate leading to Rora Farmhouse, but don't go back through it, instead take the footpath to the left and walk along the edge of the field, with oak trees to your left and a fence on your right. Keep going until the end where you go through a little kissing gate into Rora Woods.

Follow the footpath sign taking you down to the right, continue right to the bottom (other tracks will merge with yours and you will start to see the rooftops of Liverton). At the bottom there's a clearing; turn sharp right along a wide gravel path which leads you along the edge of the woods. Walk past a house with huge barns and take the footpath on your left, out of the woods and along the path, putting your dog on a lead before you reach the road. Turn left, and then left again at the T-junction. For a shorter walk you could turn right instead, heading back to Leat Cottages where you turn right to return to your car.

Follow the road over a little bridge and take the first footpath on the right, through metal gates and along a lovely securely fenced footpath across several fields. When you reach the lane turn right and continue past Leat Cottages before retracing your steps to your car.

USEFUL Information

START: Near Blackpool School, Liverton Village TQ12 6HQ.

WHAT3WORDS: rounds.belly.sprouting

TERRAIN: Fields, paths, moorland and quiet roads. It gets really muddy in the fields after rain, so this is a walk to do in dry weather!

PARKING: On road parking on the way out of Liverton towards Bickington. Past Benedict's Bridge Garage, on the right-hand side just after the Blackpool School car park entrance.

REFRESHMENTS: The Welcome Stranger Pub, a bit further along the road from the parking, is 'dog, children, cyclist and walker friendly' according to its Facebook page and has an outside patio and garden area. The Star Inn in Liverton allows dogs in their bar and outside in the garden area. There is also a lovely village post office which sells lots of local produce, perfect for a picnic or post-walk snack.

TOILETS: There are no public toilets on this route, the nearest would be a 5 minutes drive away at Stover Country Park on the Newton Abbot Road TQ12 6QG, or Station Road Bovey Tracey TQ13 9AW.

DOG BINS: In Liverton Village.

WALK 08
POUNDSGATE & SPITCHWICK

WHAT3WORDS:
CUTAWAY.MAINFRAME.ECHO

DISTANCE:
A little under 3 miles

TIME:
It takes me about 1 hour and 30 minutes

Poundsgate is quite a busy part of the moor. Although this lovely walk takes you far from the madding crowds, you do start and finish along a main road, so this walk is best if you find yourself free mid-week and out of holiday season. As soon as you leave the road via the footpath you are off the beaten track and can enjoy a tranquil walk, skirting the Spitchwick Estate, to a remote hamlet and back through attractive woodland.

36 | DOG WALKS IN DEVON

DOG WALKS IN DEVON

WALKIES

From the pub – where Arthur Conan Doyle stayed while he wrote *The Hound of the Baskervilles* – walk down the lane, passing the Old Post Office on your left. Just beyond the SLOW sign painted in the road, take a footpath on the right beside a stream, signposted Lower Town and Townwood cottages. Follow the path ahead, to the left of a waterfilled ditch, to a metal pedestrian gate which takes you out onto a drive where you turn right.

Keep on the drive past the white gates of Spitchwick Manor, an estate mentioned in the Domesday Book as one of the 72 manors in Devon held by William the Conqueror. The current manor house was constructed during the 19th Century and the gardens are occasionally open to the public; apparently there is a secret garden with a plunge pool which was built for Lady Ashburton in 1763.

Ignore a signposted footpath to the right (which we return by later) and walk on past a lovely wooden barn conversion called Woodcott and then the Estate Offices on your left. You will reach a pretty brick cottage and opposite is a footpath which takes you through a gate into a field. There were horses and sheep in the field when I last walked it, so keep your dog on a lead. They weren't at all interested so don't be nervous; they seem used to people walking through.

Follow the direction of the footpath arrows across the field to a gate, go through it and then keep to the left-hand edge of the field, through another gateway and then you reach Lower Town through a wooden gate onto a driveway, passing houses, a telephone box and a farmyard to come out onto a lane by a red post box. (I love this section as it feels like you're stepping back in time!).

Turn right and follow the road downhill, bearing left by Woodpecker Cottage, ignoring a dead-end to the right. Follow this lovely quiet lane for about ¾ of a mile, enjoying the moor and woodland views. Pass Oak Cottage and then at the bottom of the hill there's a farmhouse on the bend (there are often some noisy dogs to greet you as you pass, but they are safely enclosed!). Turn right straight after the farmhouse following a footpath sign through a big metal gate into the wood.

Stay on the stony track as it climbs up through the wood next to the brook. At the brow of the hill go through a gateway (this has always been open when I've walked this route, but there is a rickety-looking stile to the right if not!). Continue into a field, keeping to the right-hand boundary towards a pair of wooden gates. Take the left-hand gate to stay on the track heading back towards Spitchwick Manor which you will see as you get near.

At the end of the field hop over the stile onto the drive and turn left, going uphill to the metal gate and back into the first field you crossed. Walk back along the path next to the ditch until you reach the road, where you turn left and walk back uphill to the pub.

USEFUL
Information

START: By the Tavistock Inn, Poundsgate TQ13 7NY.

WHAT3WORDS: cutaway.mainframe.echo

TERRAIN: Pretty footpaths, country lanes and woodland. Might be hard going in very wet weather as there are several fields to cross. Not too strenuous but a good stretch of the legs.

PARKING: At quiet times I've been lucky enough to find on-street parking just before the pub on the left-hand side of the road. The Tavistock Inn has a car park for patrons only. You can park on the Moor before you get to the pub, which will add about a mile to the walk.

REFRESHMENTS: Dogs are welcome on leads at the Tavistock Inn, but not in the rear garden. There's usually an ice cream van at Newbridge.

TOILETS: In the car park at Newbridge, just before you get to Poundsgate (what3words: improving.partners.lamenting) and in nearby Ashburton, 4 miles away.

DOG BINS: None on this route.

SPECIAL INTEREST

THERE ARE PLENTY OF WILDFLOWERS ON THIS ROUTE; RANSOMS, PINK CAMPION, GARLIC, PRIMROSES, VIOLETS AND FOXGLOVES JUST FOR STARTERS! THE WOOD IS CARPETED WITH WHITE WOOD ANEMONES AND BLUEBELLS IN THE SPRING. KEEP AN EYE OPEN FOR DEER.

09

WALK 09
MANATON & BARROWMAN'S NOSE

WHAT3WORDS:
RESPONSES.OUTBID.IMPLANTED

DISTANCE:
2.5 miles or 3.5 miles with the loop at the end

TIME:
It takes me almost exactly an hour; the longer version adds another 25 minutes - allow extra if you want to stop and enjoy the view or have a picnic

I love this walk which combines village lanes with rugged, open moor and an interesting rock called The Barrowman's Nose. This feels like you've had a really good walk on the Moor, but it only takes about an hour – although you can extend the route by adding an extra loop behind the church at the end, which takes you to a viewpoint at Manaton Rocks.

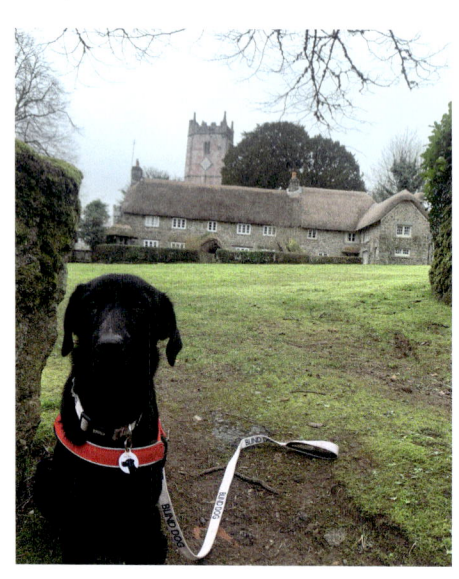

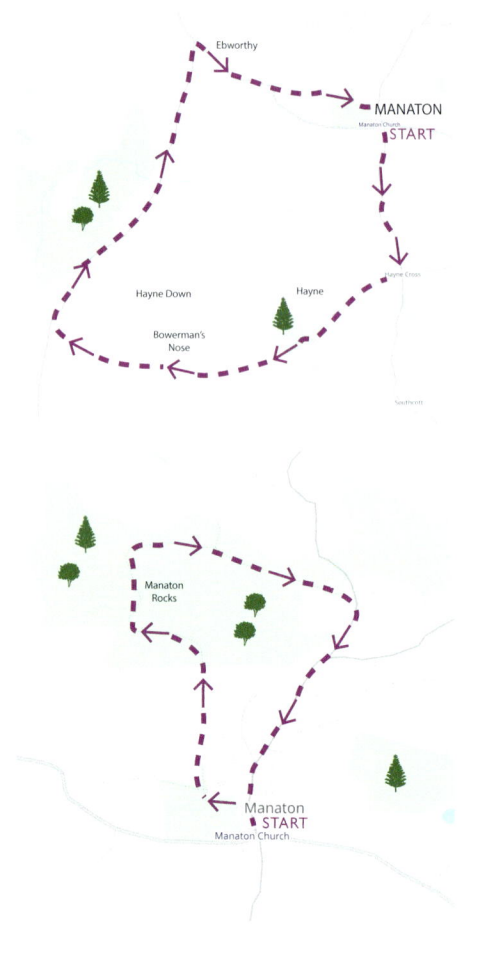

40 | DOG WALKS IN DEVON

USEFUL
Information

START: Manaton Church car park TQ13 9UJ.

WHAT3WORDS: responses.outbid.implanted

TERRAIN: There is a rocky hill climb which can be tricky, after which you descend the moor picking your way through the boulders and bracken. The rest is along footpaths and pretty country lanes. There is one stile where I need to lift Mo over as there's no easy route through for dogs; you can walk back along the road to avoid this if your furry friend is on the large side.

PARKING: Park in Manaton Village car park. There is an honesty box for the suggested £1 parking fee, so don't forget to bring some change!

REFRESHMENTS: The village pub, The Kestor Inn is dog friendly and offers a Sunday carvery. There is also a delightful stall outside the School House on the village green which sells water, flapjack and cakes as well as bread and eggs. You will need cash to buy their goodies.

TOILETS: No public toilets on this route.

DOG BINS: There are bins at Manaton next to the bus stop.

DOG WALKS IN DEVON | 41

WALKIES

Walk back to the car park entrance and cross the road, taking a narrow lane signposted to Leighon, with a blue 'unsuitable for vehicles' sign. Ignore a footpath sign on the left and then pass Mill Farm on the right. At the second five bar gate enter the field on your right which has a footpath sign to Hayne Down and Jay's Grave. Walk diagonally across the field to the stile ahead, hopping over onto Hayne Road and turn right. (If there are cows in the field and you don't fancy going through it, continue down the road and at the crossroads turn right onto Hayne Road).

This quiet road heads up to the moor, passing more footpath signs, and a house called 'Hayne' before becoming a stony footpath. Continue up the hill on this lovely old route, admiring the old stone walls and ancient trees covered in lichens and moss. Go through a wooden gate and turn immediately right, walking up onto the open moor. This is a very rocky path and it's quite a hill, so make sure you stop and admire the view back down the hill towards Manaton church while you catch your breath.

Follow the path right up to the top, walking between the big rock stacks where you will be rewarded with amazing 360° views. You can see Haytor and Hound Tor to your left and glorious sweeping views of the surrounding moor.

Keeping Manaton Church on your right with Haytor behind you, carry on Northwest through the rocks to the end of the ridge, where you start to descend on a grassy path.

Bowerman's Nose is on the right as you descend. This is a tall stack of weathered granite, which looks a bit like the profile of a man with a cap on his head. Bowerman is thought to come from the words "bow man" and legend says that a bowman was hunting and disturbed a group of witches who cursed him and turned him and his hounds into stone (hence Hound Tor which you can see in the distance).

Continue down the hill, picking your way between the rocks and bracken. You're aiming for the house with solar panels on its roof, which is called Blissmoor and is said to have been a mine captain's house. When you reach the tarmac path turn right and follow this long path, enjoying the moorland scenery as you walk towards a big white house on the horizon. It's a long lane and you go through a wooden gate halfway along. Make sure you pop your dog on a lead before you get back to the main road which you will see ahead.

Turn right towards Manaton and walk along the main road for a short while. This isn't a busy road, but you may meet one or two cars so take care. You pass Ebworthy House, which you've been looking at in the distance, and to your right you will clearly see Barrowman's Nose which now looks really small in the distance! Take the footpath left by the 'road narrows' sign, directing you to the church. (This isn't easy for dogs and I have to lift Mo over this. You can walk back round the road to the car park if it's a real problem). Cross the field, which is often full of grazing sheep, keeping to the left-hand boundary. Go through a gap in the stone wall, where you get an amazing view of Haytor. Go through the kissing gate and turn right, following the path towards the church.

Now you can choose the return to your car, either by crossing the graveyard and turning right at the village green, or you can extend the walk by turning left, signposted Langstone via Manaton Rocks. The longer route takes you past Half Moon House which was owned by Daphne Du Maurier's artist sister Jeanne and her partner, the poet Noel Welch, who left it to the National Trust when she died.

Simply follow the path, over wooden steps, up the hill, following signs to Manaton rocks. If you don't have any loose toddlers or dogs, and it's not blowing a hooley, you can climb on the rocks and admire the view across the treetops. It is high and unfenced so please tread carefully. I have had a picnic or two on top and you would be hard pressed to find a better viewpoint!

Still following a well-trodden path, take the main track down through the woods below the rocks, turning right at the junction signposted Manaton. When you reach the gate with a horseshoe fastening, turn right and follow the road back down to the village green near the church and passing the little stall of goodies at the School House, before returning to the car park.

SPECIAL INTEREST

THE EXCEPTIONAL VIEWS OF THE SURROUNDING COUNTRYSIDE ARE PERHAPS THE BEST THING ABOUT THIS WALK, AND THE DRIVE FROM BOVEY TRACEY TO MANATON IS BREATHTAKING. THE PICTURESQUE VILLAGE GREEN IS VERY CHARMING, AND IT CAN BE FUN TO TIE YOUR WALK IN WITH A VISIT TO THE VILLAGE HALL FOR THEIR MONTHLY PRODUCE MARKET. CHECK THEIR WEBSITE FOR DETAILS.

WALK 10
NORTH BOVEY & EASDON TOR

WHAT3WORDS:
MEDIATE.STRUMMING.BLOTCHY

DISTANCE:
Approximately 4.5 miles

TIME:
It takes me 2.5 hours – allow extra for picnics and to stop and enjoy the view

This is a difficult walk but definitely one of my favourites. You will really feel like you've earnt a pint in the pub at the end of it! The first section is all uphill and then you come to a wild section of the moor with incredible views – but often a biting wind! Not a walk to do in bad weather or poor visibility. You leave the moor via a lovely ancient woodland and then finally return to the village either via stepping stones or a bridge.

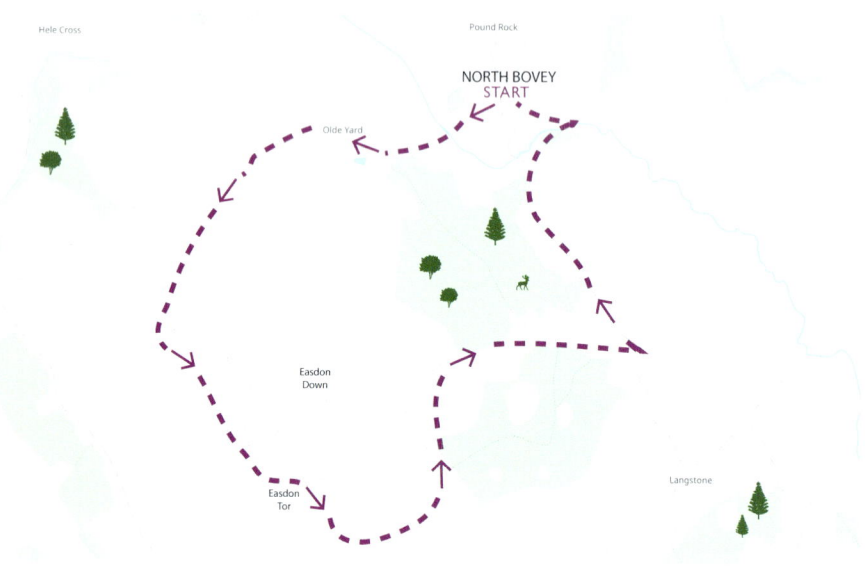

44 | DOG WALKS IN DEVON

USEFUL
Information

START: From the little free car park in North Bovey.

WHAT3WORDS: mediate.strumming.blotchy

TERRAIN: Steep country lanes to start, then a narrow, uneven footpath takes you onto open moor. The downhill through woodland is uneven and can be wet and muddy, then you return to the start along village lanes and either a pedestrian bridge or large stepping stones.

PARKING: Free car park in North Bovey and limited on-street parking by the village green.

REFRESHMENTS: The Ring of Bells is a charming, dog friendly 13th century thatched inn on the village green. The walk has plenty of places which make ideal picnic stops, so you could pack a sandwich and eat your lunch while enjoying a fabulous view!

TOILETS: The Ring of Bells has toilets for patrons only. Nearest public toilets are at Lustleigh, TQ13 9TA or Bovey Tracey, TQ13 9AW.

DOG BINS: None on the route except in the village itself.

WALKIES

Turn left out of the car park and immediately take the footpath on the right, which takes you around the churchyard. When you reach a quiet road turn left and go over the bridge which crosses the River Bovey. Keep going all the way up the hill, passing New Mill Cottages – you can still see the Mill Wheel in the garden. Pass (or have a quick rest on) a bench and ignore the paths off. Continue until you reach a lovely hamlet called Yarde, with a beautiful farmhouse and farm buildings either side of the road. Ignore the right hand turning at Yarde Cross, continuing uphill and following a signpost to Manaton. As the road flattens, look out for a little lane to the left, signposted 'Byway Langdon and Bridlepath to Easdon'. Walk up this lovely stony lane but take care as the ground is uneven. Carry on this long track, with stone walls and high hedges protecting you from the wind.

After about half a mile, as the lane starts to drop down, you take the left-hand turn and walk up to a gate. Walk through the gate and you are on the moor. If you look right up to the horizon you will see a small wind-blown tree and a trig point way above you and slightly to the right. That's where you aim for as you trudge up the hill! There are some big boulders on the way which make good seats if you're ready for a picnic or a cup of something hot. There is a fairly clear path but keep the little wind-blown tree in your sights and you won't go wrong!

As you reach the trig point, you'll see a wide grassy path to your left, which you need to take once you've admired the incredible view – from here you can see King Tor to the west, Honeybag and Chinkwell Tor to the south, and Haytor and Hound Tor to the east.

Back to the wide grassy track which takes you through the heather in an easterly direction, heading to a 'Cairn' or burial chamber on the slope of the next hill. Continue in the same direction until you see a tall rock stack, known locally as Figgie Daniel (it's not clear where this name comes from, but it may relate to a moorman who once farmed in this area). Head southeast here, down past Figgie Daniel and remaining on the narrow path until you reach the corner of an old stone wall, which is flanked by tall trees. Head left along the path, keeping the large boulder on your right. The path now begins to head towards a conifer wood, through the bracken and passing holly trees along the way.

Stay on this path without turning off until you reach the conifer wood which is surrounded by a stone wall. There's a wooden gate here, but don't go through it, instead walk around the wood keeping the wall on your right all the way along. At the corner, leave the wall behind you as the path starts to take you downhill. This is my favourite part of the walk, as the terrain changes and you walk between lovely old trees until you find yourself in an ancient woodland, following a babbling brook which criss-crosses the path all the way to the bottom of the hill. (This section can be muddy!). At the bottom of the wood you cross the stream again and go through a wooden gate, and then follow the 'path' signs down through the conifer woods, through a five-bar gate to the road.

Turn left and follow the road back to North Bovey, passing Mill Cottage and Aller Farm. Just before the beautiful old bridge, take the footpath to the right which takes you to stepping stones or a pedestrian bridge where you cross the River Bovey again. Turn left afterwards and walk all the way up the lane, ignoring a footpath across a sheep field, and make your way back to the village green. Turn left again to return to the car park.

SPECIAL INTEREST

NORTH BOVEY IS A QUINTESSENTIAL DEVON VILLAGE, WITH WHITE THATCHED COTTAGES GROUPED AROUND THE VILLAGE GREEN. THERE ARE TWENTY-SEVEN LISTED BUILDINGS INCLUDING THE CHURCH (WHICH DATES BACK TO THE 13TH CENTURY), NINETEEN COTTAGES AND THE TELEPHONE KIOSK! YOU CAN REALLY IMAGINE LIFE IN FORMER TIMES, ESPECIALLY ON THE VILLAGE GREEN WHERE YOU CAN SEE AN OLD GRANITE MOUNTING BLOCK, A WATER PUMP WITH A GRANITE TROUGH AND A MEDIEVAL CROSS, WHICH IS BACK IN ITS RIGHTFUL POSITION AFTER BEING FOUND IN THE RIVER BOVEY WHERE IT WAS BEING USED AS A STEPPING STONE! THERE IS A YEW TREE IN THE GROUNDS OF ST JOHN'S CHURCH WHICH IS HUNDREDS OF YEARS OLD.

DOG WALKS IN DEVON | 47